THE ILLUSTRATED
PICTURE
ATLAS
OF THE
WORLD

Illustrations: Gary Hincks and Steve Noon
Cover design: Katy Wall
Prepress: Splitting Image

The Illustrated Picture Atlas of the World
© 2002 Orpheus Books Ltd
First published as The Picture Atlas of the World in 2004 by Orpheus Books

Published in 2007 by Hinkler Books Pty Ltd
45–55 Fairchild Street
Heatherton VIC 3202 Australia
www.hinklerbooks.com

4 6 8 10 9 7 5 3
12 11 10 09 08

ISBN 978 1 7418 1275 6

Printed and bound in Malaysia

THE ILLUSTRATED
PICTURE
ATLAS
OF THE
WORLD

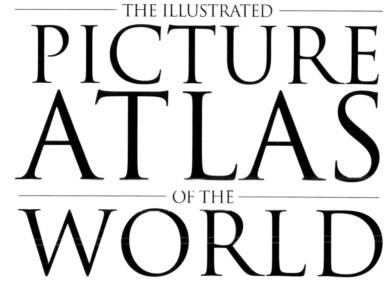

Written and designed by
Nicholas Harris

Illustrated by
Gary Hincks
&
Steve Noon

HB
HINKLER
BOOKS

CONTENTS

KEY TO ILLUSTRATIONS
Left-hand column, top Cheese-porters, Alkmaar market, The Netherlands centre Arches National Park, Utah, USA bottom Sydney Harbour Bridge and Opera House, Australia Right-hand page, top Elephant mask, Cameroon centre Royal palace, Bangkok, Thailand bottom Machu Picchu, Peru Along bottom of page The Kremlin, Moscow, Russia

ABBREVIATIONS AND
SYMBOLS USED IN THIS ATLAS

Br.	(Great) Britain
Fr.	France
I.	Island
Is.	Islands
km	kilometres
L.	Lake
m	metres
Mt.	Mount
Mts.	Mountains
Neths.	Netherlands
Pop.	Population
Port.	Portugal
Rep.	Republic
sq km	square kilometres
U.A.E.	United Arab Emirates
U.S.	United States
★	National capital
④	Numbers in circles show where the subjects illustrated can be found on the maps

THE WORLD

Wrangel I.

Ellesmere I.

Greenland

Baffin Bay

Victoria I.

Baffin I.

Iceland

Mackenzie

Hudson Bay

B

Bering Sea

Rocky Mountains

Aleutian Is.

N O R T H

St. Lawrence

Newfoundland

Missouri

A M E R I C A

PACIFIC OCEAN

Mississippi

Azores

Bermuda

ATLANTIC

Hawaiian Is.

OCEAN

Canary Is.

Gulf of Mexico

Caribbean Sea

West Indies

Cape Verde Is.

Marshall Is.

Equator

Kiribati

Galápagos Is.

Amazon

Asce

Samoa

American Samoa

Pitcairn I.

S O U T H

Fiji

Tonga

Cook Is.

French Polynesia

Easter I.

A M E R I C A

Andes

Paraná

New Zealand

Trista Cun

Andes

FACTS ABOUT THE WORLD

Circumference at the Equator 40,075 km

Land area 148,328,100 sq km

Ocean area 361,741,000 sq km

Population 6,464,750,000

Highest point Mt. Everest (Nepal and China) 8,863 m

Greatest depth Marianas Trench 10,924 m

Lowest point on land Dead Sea (Israel/Jordan) 395 m below sea level

Longest river Nile (Africa) 6,670 km

Largest lake Caspian Sea 371,000 sq km

Largest country Russia 17,075,400 sq km

Largest population China 1,315,844,000

Largest city Tokyo (Japan) 35,200,000 people

Falkland Is.

South Georgia

ARCTIC OCEAN

Severnaya
Zemlya

Svalbard

Novaya
Zemlya

Norwegian
Sea

Ob

Yenisey

Lena

Sea of
Okhotsk

North
Sea

EUROPE

Volga

Gobi

Amur

Irtysh

Kuril Is

Black Sea

Caspian
Sea

ASIA

Honshu

Mediterranean
Sea

PACIFIC

Dead
Sea

Himalayas

Mt.
Everest

Yangtse

OCEAN

a h a r a

Nile

South
China
Sea

Northern
Mariana
Is.

Arabian
Sea

Bay of
Bengal

Niger

AFRICA

Philippine
Is.

Marianas
Trench

Gulf of
Guinea

Congo

Maldive
Is.

Borneo

Palau

Marshall
Is.

Sumatra

New Guinea

Nauru

Seychelles

Java

Solomon
Is.

Cocos
I.

Madagascar

Vanuatu

Helena

Mauritius

Réunion

INDIAN

OCEAN

AUSTRALIA

New
Caledonia

Tasman
Sea

New
Zealand

Kergeulen
Is.

SOUTHERN OCEAN

ANTARCTICA

UNITED KINGDOM

ICELAND

NORWAY

SWEDEN

FINLAND

DENMARK

POLAND

GERMANY

AUSTRIA

IRELAND

NETHERLANDS

BELGIUM

LUXEMBOURG

FRANCE

SWITZERLAND

MONACO

ITALY

VATICAN CITY

SAN MARINO

MALTA

ANDORRA

PORTUGAL

SPAIN

LIECHTENSTEIN

HUNGARY

BULGARIA

ALBANIA

GREECE

SLOVENIA

CROATIA

MACEDONIA

EUROPE

EUROPE and Asia together form one vast land mass called Eurasia. Europe itself lies west of the Ural Mountains, to the north of the Caucasus and on the western bank of the Bosporus strait. A large portion of Russia, the part where most of its people live, and a small area of Turkey both fall within the area of Europe.

Europe is a land of peninsulas and islands. Their shores are lapped by the waters of the North Atlantic Ocean and its seas. Apart from the mountain ranges and the frozen Arctic lands, nearly every corner of the continent has been shaped by humans. Farmland competes for space with towns and cities, roads, airports, quarries or factories. Europe is densely populated, particularly in the lowlands of the western countries where industrial cities have grown up close to one another.

ICELAND

Fishing

Bearded seal

FAEROE IS.
(Denmark)

Killer whale

Fishing

Whisky distillery

Oil

Ski

NORTH SEA

Pigs

Sheep

Pigs

IRELAND

UNITED KINGDOM

DENM...

Cattle

Fishing

Coal

Gas

NETHERLANDS

Cattle

Channel Tunnel

BELGIUM

Kiel

LUXEMBOURG

Industry

GERMANY

Cattle

Sugar beet

Beer

Wheat

Grapes

Skiing

FRANCE

SWITZERLAND

Tobacco

Car factory

Pigs

ANDORRA

Grapes

Grape harvest

Whe...

PORTUGAL

Fishing

Sheep

Grapes

Gra...

ATLANTIC OCEAN

SPAIN

Tourism

Sheep

Oranges

GIBRALTAR (Br.)

Tourism

MEDITERRANEAN SEA

Lemons

CZECH REPUBLIC

SLOVAKIA

Mining

Lapp herdsman

White
Sea

Mining

Elk

FINLAND

L.
Ladoga

Timber

VEDEN

Mechanical
log cutter

Wolf

RUSSIA

Brown bear

Mining

ESTONIA

Oil

Aircraft
factory

Potatoes

LATVIA

Cattle

Wheat

BALTIC SEA

Cattle

LITHUANIA

Flax

Volga

RUSSIA

BELARUS

Maize

Potatoes

Sugar
beet

Potatoes

Pigs

Potatoes

POLAND

Chernobyl Nuclear
power station

Herding cattle

Caspian
Sea

heat

Coal

Horse-drawn
plough

U K R A I N E

Coal

Tobacco

REPUBLIC

Harvesting wheat

Mining

SLOVAKIA

Grapes

STRIA

Gas

Sheep

Elbrus

HUNGARY

Pigs

MOLDOVA

NIA

Wheat

Herding cattle

CROATIA

ROMANIA

Ferry

BLACK SEA

BOSNIA AND
HERZEGOVINA

SERBIA

Sheep

Grapes

Grapes

MONTENEGRO

BULGARIA

T U R K E Y

ALY

Olives

MACEDONIA

Tobacco

ALBANIA

Aegean
Sea

GREECE

Olives

Tourism

CYPRUS

FACTS ABOUT EUROPE

Area 9,700,000 sq km
Population 728,389,000
Highest point Elbrus (Russia) 5,664 m
Lowest point Caspian Sea (Russia) 28 m below sea level
Longest river Volga (Russia) 3,668 km
Largest lake Ladoga (Russia) 17,700 sq km
Largest country (excluding Russia) Ukraine 603,700 sq km
Largest population (excluding Russia) Germany 82,689,000
Largest city Moscow (Russia) 10,700,000 people

RUSSIA

ESTONIA

LATVIA

LITHUANIA

BELARUS

UKRAINE

MOLDOVA

ROMANIA

THE EUROPEAN UNION

The 27 member nations are Austria, Belgium,
Bulgaria, Cyprus, Czech Republic, Denmark,
Estonia, Finland, France, Germany, Greece, Hungary,
Ireland, Italy, Latvia, Lithuania, Luxembourg, Malta,
Poland, Portugal, Romania, Slovakia, Slovenia,
Spain, Sweden, Netherlands and United Kingdom.

MONTENEGRO

BOSNIA & HERZEGOVINA

CYPRUS

SERBIA

NATIONS OF EUROPE

ALBANIA
Area 27,398 sq km **Population** 3,130,000
Capital Tiranë **Language** Albanian

ANDORRA
Area 468 sq km **Population** 67,000 **Capital**
Andorra **Languages** Catalan, French, Spanish

AUSTRIA
Area 83,859 sq km **Population** 8,189,000
Capital Vienna **Language** German

BELARUS
Area 207,600 sq km **Population** 9,755,000
Capital Minsk **Language** Belorussian

BELGIUM
Area 30,519 sq km **Population** 10,419,000
Capital Brussels **Languages** Dutch (Flemish),
French, German

BOSNIA AND HERZEGOVINA
Area 51,129 sq km **Population** 3,907,000
Capital Sarajevo **Language** Serbo-Croat

BULGARIA
Area 110,994 sq km **Population** 7,726,000
Capital Sofia **Languages** Bulgarian, Turkish,
Macedonian

▲ Irish boy ⑥

CROATIA
Area 56,538 sq km **Population** 4,551,000
Capital Zagreb **Language** Serbo-Croat

CYPRUS
Area 9,251 sq km **Population** 835,000
Capital Nicosia **Languages** Greek, Turkish,
English

CZECH REPUBLIC
Area 78,864 sq km **Population** 10,220,000
Capital Prague **Language** Czech

DENMARK
Area 43,093 sq km **Population** 5,431,000
Capital Copenhagen **Language** Danish

ESTONIA
Area 45,125 sq km **Population** 1,330,000
Capital Tallinn **Languages** Estonian, Russian

FINLAND
Area 338,145 sq km **Population** 5,249,000
Capital Helsinki **Languages** Finnish, Swedish

FRANCE
Area 543,965 sq km **Population** 60,496,000
Capital Paris **Language** French

GERMANY
Area 356,854 sq km **Population** 82,689,000
Capital Berlin **Language** German

GREECE
Area 131,957 sq km **Pop.** 11,120,000
Capital Athens **Language** Greek

HUNGARY
Area 93,030 sq km **Population** 10,098,000
Capital Budapest **Language** Hungarian

ITALY
Area 301,277 sq km **Pop.** 58,093,000
Capital Rome **Language** Italian

LATVIA
Area 64,589 sq km **Population** 2,307,000
Capital Riga **Languages** Latvian, Russian

▶ Sami (Lapp) boy ①

▶ Gypsy girl ⑤

ICELAND
Area 103,000 sq km **Population** 295,000
Capital Reykjavik **Language** Icelandic

IRELAND
Area 70,283 sq km **Population** 4,148,000
Capital Dublin **Languages** English, Irish

LIECHTENSTEIN
Area 160 sq km **Population** 35,000
Capital Vaduz **Language** German

LITHUANIA
Area 65,200 sq km **Population** 3,431,0
Capital Vilnius **Languages** Lithuanian,
Russian, Polish, Belorussian

LUXEMBOURG
Area 2,586 sq km **Population** 465,000
Capital Luxembourg **Languages** German,
Letzeburgesch, French

MACEDONIA
Area 25,713 sq km **Pop.** 2,034,000
Capital Skopje **Languages** Macedonian,
Albanian

MOLDOVA
Area 33,700 sq km **Population** 4,206,000
Capital Kishinev **Languages** Romanian
(Moldovan), Ukrainian, Russian

MONACO
Area 2 sq km **Population** 35,000
Language French

▶ Lithuanian girl ②

NETHERLANDS
Area 33,936 sq km **Population** 16,299,000
Capitals Amsterdam, The Hague
Language Dutch

NORWAY
Area 323,877 sq km **Population** 4,620,000
Capital Oslo **Language** Norwegian

POLAND
Area 312,683 sq km **Population** 38,530,000
Capital Warsaw **Language** Polish

PORTUGAL
Area 92,389 sq km **Population** 10,495,000
Capital Lisbon **Language** Portuguese

ROMANIA
Area 237,500 sq km **Population** 21,711,000
Capital Bucharest **Languages** Romanian,
Hungarian, German

RUSSIA
Area 17,075,400 sq km **Population**
143,202,000 **Capital** Moscow
Languages Russian, 38 other languages

SAN MARINO
Area 60.5 sq km **Population** 28,000
Language Italian

SERBIA
Area 88,361 sq km **Population** 9,396,000
Capital Belgrade **Languages** Serbo-Croat,
Albanian, Hungarian

SLOVAKIA
Area 49,035 sq km **Population** 5,401,000
Capital Bratislava **Languages** Slovak,
Hungarian, Czech

SLOVENIA
Area 20,251 sq km **Population** 1,967,000
Capital Ljubljana **Language** Slovene

SPAIN
Area 504,782 sq km **Population** 43,064,000
Capital Madrid **Languages** Spanish, Catalan,
Basque, Galician

▲ Ukrainian girl ③

SWEDEN
Area 449,964 sq km **Population** 9,041,000
Capital Stockholm **Languages** Swedish, Finnish,
Lappish

SWITZERLAND
Area 41,293 sq km **Population** 7,252,000
Capital Bern **Languages** German, French,
Italian

UKRAINE
Area 603,700 sq km **Population** 46,481,000
Capital Kiev **Languages** Ukrainian, Russian

UNITED KINGDOM
Area 242,533 sq km **Population** 59,668,000
Capital London **Languages** English, Welsh

VATICAN CITY
Area 0.44 sq km **Pop.** 783 **Language** Italian

▶ Slovak boy ④

MALTA
Area 316 sq km **Population** 402,000
Capital Valletta **Languages** Maltese,
English, Italian

MONTENEGRO
Area 14,026 sq km **Population** 630,000
Capitals Podgorica **Languages** Serbo-
Croat, Albanian, Hungarian

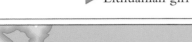

12

NORTHERN EUROPE

NORWAY, Sweden and Denmark are often grouped under the name Scandinavia. Taken together with Finland and Iceland, these are the Nordic countries of Europe.

The far north is sometimes known as the "Land of the Midnight Sun". During the summer months, the sun never goes down, the snows melt and the Lapps graze their reindeer on the grasslands. In winter, the sun never rises. The soil freezes over and the reindeer return to the forests.

Iceland, on the edge of the Arctic Ocean, is a bleak, treeless landscape of volcanoes, rock and ice caps.

▲ A view of Stockholm, capital city of Sweden. ①

▲ Reindeer graze in Lapland's summer pastures. ②

▲ A glassblower makes glasses in Sweden. ②

HAMMERFEST

Inari ②

LAPLAND

TROMSØ

NARVIK

KIRUNA

OULU

LULEÅ

VAASA

FINLAND

KUOPIO

UMEÅ

ÖSTERSUND

TRONDHEIM

Lofoten Is.

Gulf of Bothnia

NORWEGIAN SEA

ICELAND

AKUREYRI

Vatnajökull

REYKJAVIK

Scale
0   150 km

▲ More than 1,000 years ago, the Vikings sailed from Scandinavia in search of new lands. They reached North America. This carving is of a Viking warrior. ④

▼ Legoland in Denmark is an exhibition of models made of plastic bricks. ⑥

Map labels:

LAHTI
• HELSINKI
Gulf of Finland
TURKU
TALLINN L. Peipus
ESTONIA
RIGA
L A T V I A
KAUNAS
VILNIUS
L I T H U A N I A
Saaremaa
LIEPAJA
Åland Is.
UPPSALA ①
STOCKHOLM
④
Gotland
VISBY
Öland
B A L T I C   S E A
KARLSKRONA
③
NORRKÖPING
Vättern
KARLSTAD
GÖTEBORG
COPENHAGEN
MALMÖ
Vänern
Bornholm
OSLO
N
ÅLBORG
ÅRHUS
ODENSE
D E N M A R K
⑥
Skagerrak
KRISTIANSAND
STAVANGER
BERGEN

▲ Down the west coast of Norway, long fingers of the sea reach deep inland. These are called fjords. On either side, mountain slopes rise steeply out of the water.

Tens of thousands of years ago, Scandinavia lay under a vast sheet of ice. Rivers of ice, called glaciers, carved deep valleys in the mountains. When the glaciers melted, the sea flooded in. The valleys became fjords.

Norway's coastline is so jagged that, if it were straightened out, it would reach halfway round the world! ⑤

BRITISH ISLES

THE BRITISH ISLES is the name given to the group of islands that lie off the northwestern coast of Europe. The two largest islands are Great Britain ("Little Britain" is Brittany in France) and Ireland. The United Kingdom consists of Great Britain, which includes England, Scotland and Wales, and Northern Ireland. The north and west are mostly highland. Central and southern Britain are more low-lying, a mixture of rolling farmland and cities.

The sea has played an important part in Britain's history. Traders and settlers travelled by sea to distant parts of the globe and Britain built up one of the largest empires the world has ever seen.

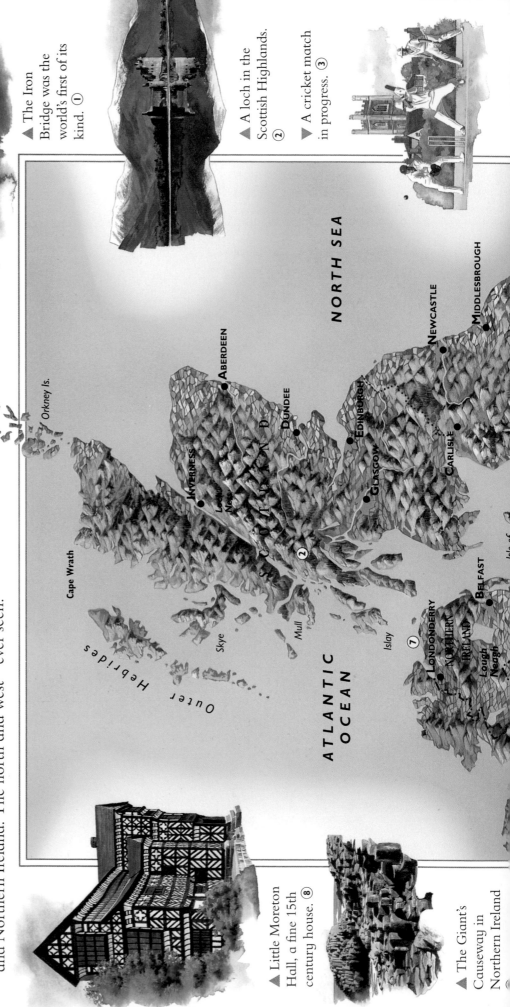

▲ The Iron Bridge was the world's first of its kind. ①

▲ A loch in the Scottish Highlands. ②

▼ A cricket match in progress. ③

▲ Little Moreton Hall, a fine 15th century house. ⑧

▲ The Giant's Causeway in Northern Ireland

NORTH SEA

ATLANTIC OCEAN

Shetland Is.

Orkney Is.

Cape Wrath

Outer Hebrides

Skye

Mull

Islay

SCOTLAND

INVERNESS

Loch Ness

ABERDEEN

DUNDEE

GLASGOW

EDINBURGH

CARLISLE

NEWCASTLE

MIDDLESBROUGH

BELFAST

LONDONDERRY

NORTHERN IRELAND

Lough Neagh

② ⑦

14

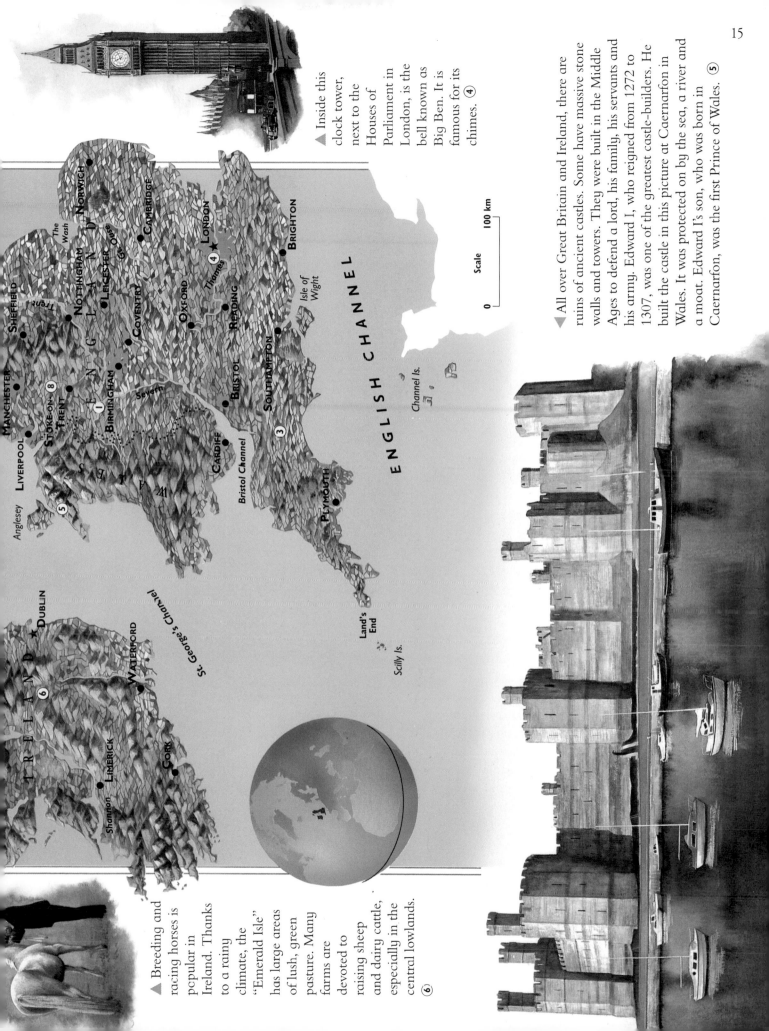

▲ Inside this clock tower, next to the Houses of Parliament in London, is the bell known as Big Ben. It is famous for its chimes. ④

▼ All over Great Britain and Ireland, there are ruins of ancient castles. Some have massive stone walls and towers. They were built in the Middle Ages to defend a lord, his family, his servants and his army. Edward I, who reigned from 1272 to 1307, was one of the greatest castle-builders. He built the castle in this picture at Caernarfon in Wales. It was protected on by the sea, a river and a moat. Edward I's son, who was born in Caernarfon, was the first Prince of Wales. ⑤

▲ Breeding and racing horses is popular in Ireland. Thanks to a rainy climate, the "Emerald Isle" has large areas of lush, green pasture. Many farms are devoted to raising sheep and dairy cattle, especially in the central lowlands. ⑥

Scale

0   100 km

IRELAND ⑥

DUBLIN ★

WATERFORD

LIMERICK

Shannon

CORK

St. George's Channel

ENGLAND

Anglesey

The Wash

LIVERPOOL

MANCHESTER

SHEFFIELD

NOTTINGHAM

Trent

LEICESTER

Gt. Ouse

NORWICH

CAMBRIDGE

STOKE-ON-TRENT ⑧

BIRMINGHAM ①

COVENTRY

Severn

OXFORD

LONDON ★ ④

Thames

READING

BRIGHTON

BRISTOL

CARDIFF

Bristol Channel

SOUTHAMPTON ③

Isle of Wight

PLYMOUTH

Land's End

Scilly Is.

Channel Is.

ENGLISH CHANNEL

⑤ ⑦

FRANCE

FRANCE is the largest country in western Europe. Warm, wet weather is good for the pastures and orchards of Brittany and Normandy in the north-west. Eastern France can be hot in summer but very cold in winter. The south is warm enough all year round for grapes, tobacco and olive trees to grow.

▲ This man is using the keen nose of a pig to hunt for truffles, a kind of mushroom. ①

▲ This train is known as the TGV, short for Train à Grande Vitesse (high-speed train). It is the fastest train in the world, holding the speed record of 515 km/h. Since it first ran in 1981, new, straight tracks have been built for it all over France. Every journey is controlled by computers. ⑦

▲ The abbey of Mont-St-Michel stands on an old hill just off the coast of Normandy. You can go there by road, but at high tide it is surrounded by the sea! ⑥

Scale

0   100 km

BAY OF BISCAY

CA

AMIE

ROUEN

LE HAVRE

PAR

NORMANDY

BREST

BRITTANY

⑥

RENNES

⑦   LE MANS

ORLE

TOURS

Loire

Cher

NANTES

POITIERS

Vienne

LA ROCHELLE

LIMOGES

①

BORDEAUX   Dordogne ②

Lot

GASCONY

⑤

BIARRITZ   TOULO

Garonne

Pyrenees

◀ The cave paintings at Lascaux are 17,000 years old. ②

◀ The Eiffel Tower was built for the Paris exhibition in 1889. It was then the tallest building in the world. Standing 301 metres tall, it was nearly twice the height of the next tallest, the Washington Monument. In hot weather, it grows by another 18 cm as the metal expands. It took 230 men just over two years to build the tower. The 18,000 pieces of iron were hammered together using 2.5 million rivets.

At first, many people thought the Eiffel Tower ugly and unsafe. Now it is one of the best-known landmarks in the world. ③

▲ France was once part of the Roman empire. The Romans constructed many magnificent roads and buildings. Still standing today is this aqueduct, called the Pont du Gard. It was built outside Nîmes nearly 2,000 years ago. It used to carry water into the city from nearby hills. ④

◀ The Tour de France is the world's greatest bicycle race. For three weeks in July, hundreds of riders speed through the French country-side (and often through neigh-bouring countries as well). ⑤

MEDITERRANEAN SEA

CORSICA
Ajaccio

THE NETHERLANDS

NEARLY ALL of the Netherlands is completely flat. One third of the land actually lies below the level of the sea. Sand dunes, earth embankments called dykes and sea walls keep the seawater from flooding in. Many areas once actually lay under water. People dug ditches and built windmills to pump the water away along

canals. In this way, they reclaimed the land from the sea. These polderlands, as they are called, are used for farmland and pasture.

The Netherlands are sometimes known as Holland, although this name really refers only to one part of the country. It is one of the most densely populated nations in the world.

▲ Windmills and canals are found all over the Dutch countryside. ①

▲ The Skinny Bridge in Amsterdam. ②

▲ Carrying cheeses to market in Alkmaar. ③

▲ Rotterdam, situated near the mouth of the River Rhine, is the busiest port in the world. ⑧

NETHERLANDS

GRONINGEN

LEEUWARDEN

ENSCHEDE

ZWOLLE

APELDOORN

ARNHEM

NIJMEGEN

Maas

IJsselmeer

Wadden Sea

Frisian Islands

Lek

Waal

UTRECHT

AMSTERDAM ★ ②

③ ALKMAAR

DEN HELDER

⑦

EINDHOVEN

TILBURG

BREDA

DORDRECHT ①

⑧ ROTTERDAM

LEIDEN

HAARLEM

THE HAGUE ★

Rhine-Maas Delta

NORTH SEA

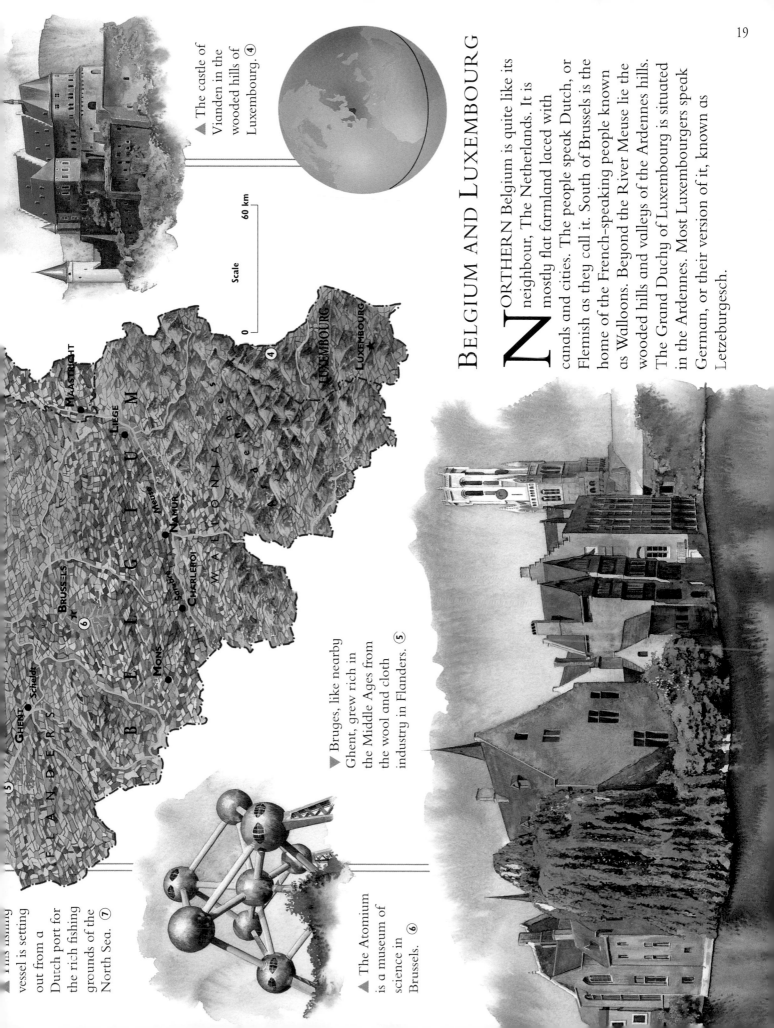

BELGIUM AND LUXEMBOURG

NORTHERN Belgium is quite like its neighbour, The Netherlands. It is mostly flat farmland laced with canals and cities. The people speak Dutch, or Flemish as they call it. South of Brussels is the home of the French-speaking people known as Walloons. Beyond the River Meuse lie the wooded hills and valleys of the Ardennes hills. The Grand Duchy of Luxembourg is situated in the Ardennes. Most Luxembourgers speak German, or their version of it, known as Letzeburgesch.

▲ The castle of Vianden in the wooded hills of Luxembourg. ④

▶ Bruges, like nearby Ghent, grew rich in the Middle Ages from the wool and cloth industry in Flanders. ⑤

▲ The Atomium is a museum of science in Brussels. ⑥

This fishing vessel is setting out from a Dutch port for the rich fishing grounds of the North Sea. ⑦

Scale

0   60 km

PORTUGAL

NOWHERE in Portugal is very far from the sea. More than 500 years ago, men from Portugal set off to cross the oceans and explore the continents of Africa and Asia. Today, sea fishing and tourism are important industries. Portugal is also famous for its cork trees and a sweet wine, called port.

◀ This is Portuguese fishing boat is called a moliceiro. ①

▶ A woman from a small village in southern Portugal. ②

▲ This is the Dom Luis Bridge. It crosses the Douro River as it flows through the city of Porto, Portugal's second largest city. Cars can drive on both upper and lower roadways. ⑥

▶ These windmills stand on the plains of La Mancha in central Spain to the south of the capital, Madrid. In a famous Spanish tale, an old knight called Don Quixote mistakes the windmills for giants. He even rode his horse into battle against them! ⑤

ATLANTIC OCEAN

A CORUÑA

GALICIA

SANTANDER

BILB

Sil

LEÓN

VIGO

OLD CASTILE

BUF

VALLADOLID

Duer

⑥

PORTO

Douro

SALAMANCA

①

S   P   A

COIMBRA

③

MADRID ★

NEW CAST

Tagus

TOLEDO

P
O
R
T
U
G
A
L

Guadiana

②

CIUDAD REAL

⑤

LISBON ★

BADAJOZ

CÓRDOBA   Guadalquivir

A   N   D   A   L   U   C   I   A

ALGARVE

SEVILLA

GRANADA   ④

Sierra Nev

MÁLAGA

CÁDIZ

GIBRALTAR (Br.)

▶ Spanish kings lived at El Escorial 400 years ago. Their empire included much of America. ③

SPAIN

ONLY a few miles of sea lies between Spain and north-west Africa. In the south, the climate is similar: hot and dry in summer. The north of the country is wetter and greener. Not all the people in Spain speak Spanish. The Basques, Galicians and Catalans have their own languages.

DONOSTIA

BASQUE PROVINCES

Pyrenees

ANDORRA

ARAGON

ZARAGOZA   LLEIDA

Ebro   CATALONIA

BARCELONA

N

Scale
0   100 km

Menorca

CUENCA

Mallorca

PALMA

VALENCIA

Júcar

Eivissa
(Ibiza)

ALBACETE

ALACANT

MURCIA

MEDITERRANEAN
SEA

CARTAGENA

▲ Arab people from Africa, called the Moors, once ruled Spain. They were driven out of Spain more than 500 years ago. They left behind them great palaces, castles and mosques (their places of worship). The Alhambra was a Moorish palace built on a hill in the city of Granada. This illustration shows the Court of Lions in the Alhambra. It was named after the carved lion statues around the fountain. ④

GERMANY

Flat northern Germany is part of the North European Plain. Travel east and the first uplands you come to are the Urals in Russia. Go south, and you will cross a landscape of wooded hills and fertile valleys. Eventually, at the Austrian border, you will reach the towering peaks of the Alps.

Germany became a single country for the first time in 1871. Before then, Germans lived in a land divided into a patchwork of duchies, principalities and kingdoms. It was divided into East and West after World War Two in 1945, but became one country again in 1990, with its capital once more in Berlin.

▲ Berlin was once divided by a wall. Now people can walk through the Brandenburg Gate. ①

▲ Riverboats steer through the Rhine gorge, a land of vine-covered slopes and hilltop castles. ②

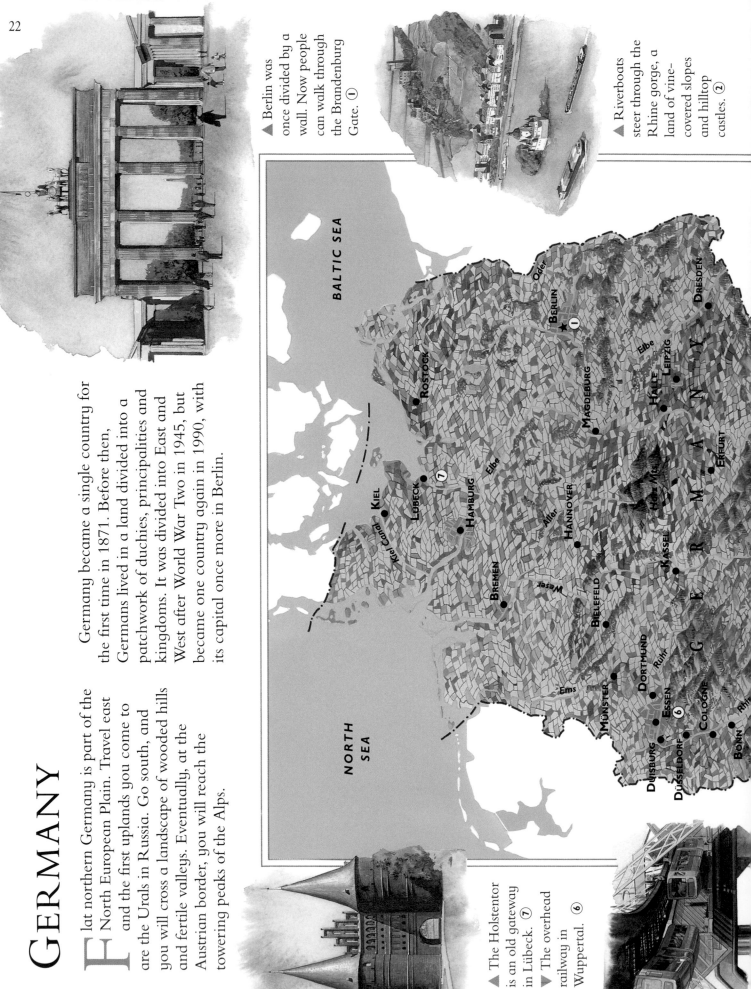

BALTIC SEA

NORTH SEA

Oder
BERLIN ★ ①
ROSTOCK
Elbe
MAGDEBURG
LEIPZIG
HALLE
DRESDEN
LÜBECK ⑦
KIEL
Kiel Canal
HAMBURG
Elbe
EFURT
Aller
HANNOVER
Harz Mts.
BREMEN
Weser
KASSEL
BIELEFELD
G E R M A N Y
Ems
MÜNSTER
DORTMUND
Ruhr
ESSEN ⑥
DUISBURG
DÜSSELDORF
COLOGNE
BONN
Rhine

▲ The Holstentor is an old gateway in Lübeck. ⑦
▶ The overhead railway in Wuppertal. ⑥

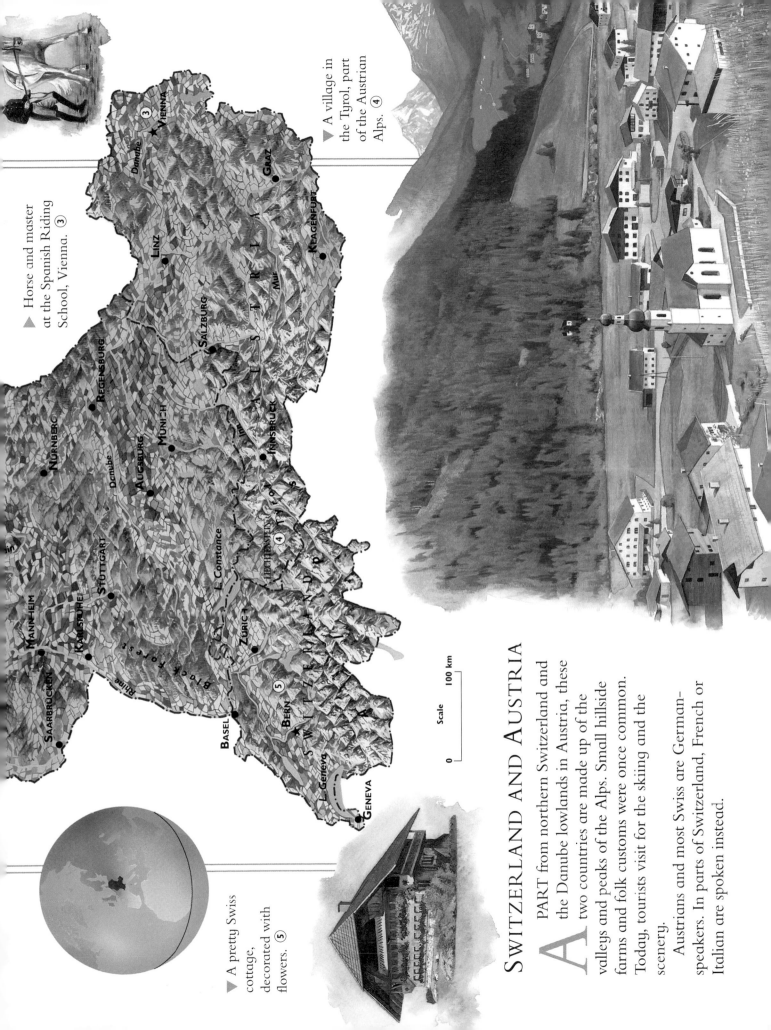

△ Horse and master at the Spanish Riding School, Vienna. ③

▶ A village in the Tyrol, part of the Austrian Alps. ④

▶ A pretty Swiss cottage, decorated with flowers. ⑤

VIENNA ③
Danube
LINZ
GRAZ
Mur
KLAGENFURT
SALZBURG
A U S T R I A
INNSBRUCK
REGENSBURG
NÜRNBERG
AUGSBURG
MUNICH
Danube
STUTTGART
KARLSRUHE
MANNHEIM
SAARBRÜCKEN
Black Forest
Rhine
LIECHTENSTEIN ④
L. Constance
ZÜRICH
BASEL
S W I T Z E R L A N D
BERN ⑤
A
L. Geneva
GENEVA

Scale
0   100 km

SWITZERLAND AND AUSTRIA

APART from northern Switzerland and the Danube lowlands in Austria, these two countries are made up of the valleys and peaks of the Alps. Small hillside farms and folk customs were once common. Today, tourists visit for the skiing and the scenery.

Austrians and most Swiss are German-speakers. In parts of Switzerland, French or Italian are spoken instead.

24

ITALY

POINTING out into the Mediterranean Sea, Italy is shaped like a boot. It looks as if it is about to kick the island of Sicily! All around Italy's northern borders are the Alps. These high, craggy mountains separate the country from the rest of Europe. Lower mountains, called the Apennines,

run the length of the boot, all the way down to the "toe" in the south.

Away from the high ground, Italy has a warm climate. Grapevines, olives and fruit trees grow all over the country. In the flat, fertile plain of the River Po, farmers grow a special type of wheat, called durum. It is used to make pasta.

▲ Venice is built on an island in a shallow bay. Canals are its streets, gondolas its taxis. ①

▲ The Dolomites are a range of jagged peaks. ②

▶ A cardinal, a churchman from Vatican City State. ③

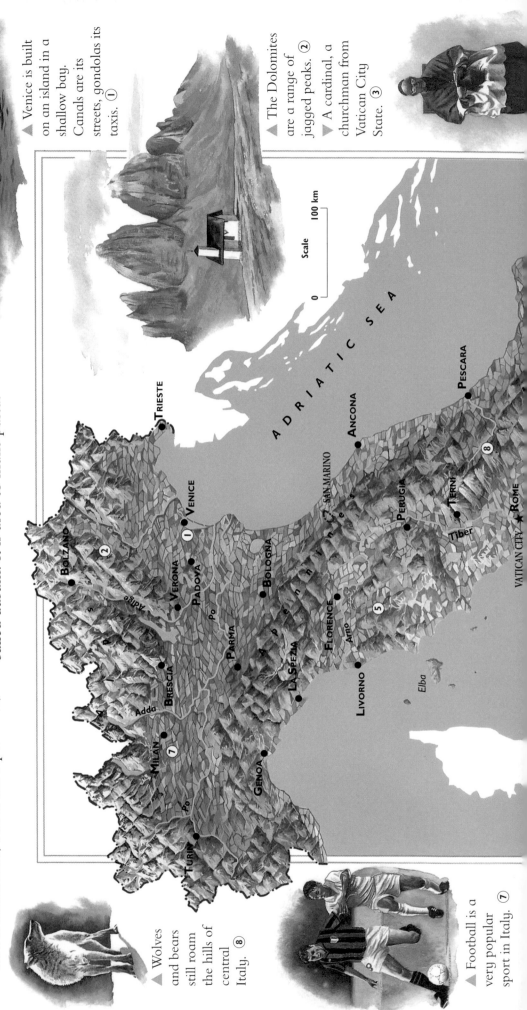

Scale

0 — 100 km

ADRIATIC SEA

TRIESTE

PESCARA

ANCONA

VENICE ①

SAN MARINO ⑦

PERUGIA

TERNI ⑧

BOLZANO ②

VERONA

PADOVA

BOLOGNA

Po

Adige

FLORENCE

Arno

Tiber

ROME

VATICAN CITY ★

PARMA

LA SPEZIA

LIVORNO

Elba

⑤

BRESCIA

Adda

MILAN ⑦

Po

GENOA

TURIN

Po

Apennines

Alps

▲ Wolves and bears still roam the hills of central Italy. ⑧

▲ Football is a very popular sport in Italy. ⑦

25

▶ These are the ruins of Pompeii, a Roman town buried in ash when Vesuvius erupted in AD 79. ④

▼ San Gimignano, a small town in Tuscany, central Italy, is famous for its towers. Only 15 remain out of the 72 originally built more than 600 years ago. ⑤

▲ Known as *trulli*, these peculiar houses in the southern Italian town of Alberobello are shaped like pepperpots. Their roofs are built from stone slabs. ⑥

BRINDISI ⑥
TARANTO
SALERNO
Vesuvius
④
NAPLES
REGGIO DI CALABRIA
MESSINA
CATANIA
Etna
Stromboli
PALERMO
SICILY
VALLETTA
MALTA
Pantelleria
SASSARI
CAGLIARI
SARDINIA
TYRRHENIAN SEA
MEDITERRANEAN SEA

EASTERN EUROPE

TRAVELLING east from Germany, the North European Plain fans out to meet the shores of the Black Sea in the south. Apart from the forested Carpathian Mountains, much of the land is intensively farmed. Ukraine, with its "black earth", has the most fertile land in the region.

▲ In Eastern Europe, traditional costumes are worn for important occasions. This couple are at a wedding in Slovakia. ⑦

▼ Prague Castle stands on a hill overlooking the Czech capital city. Inside its walls, you will find a cathedral, palaces, narrow, winding streets, and squares. St. Vaclav, "Good King Wenceslas", is buried here. ⑥

◄ All over Eastern Europe, people live and work on small farms. Animals like chickens, pigs and these geese are valuable possessions. ①

BALTIC SEA

KALININGRAD
PART OF RUSSIA
GDANSK
SZCZECIN
BIAŁYSTOK
Vistula
Bug
POZNAN
P O L A N D
WARSAW
BREST
Pripet M.
LODZ
Oder
WROCLAW
PRAGUE ⑥
④
CZECH REPUBLIC
KATOWICE
KRAKÓW
BRNO
②
S L O V A K I A
Carpathian Mts.
L'VIV
Dniest
BRATISLAVA ⑦
KOŠICE
DEBRECEN
BUDAPEST ①
H U N G A R Y
L. Balaton
Danube
SZEGED
PÉCS

Scale
0   200 km

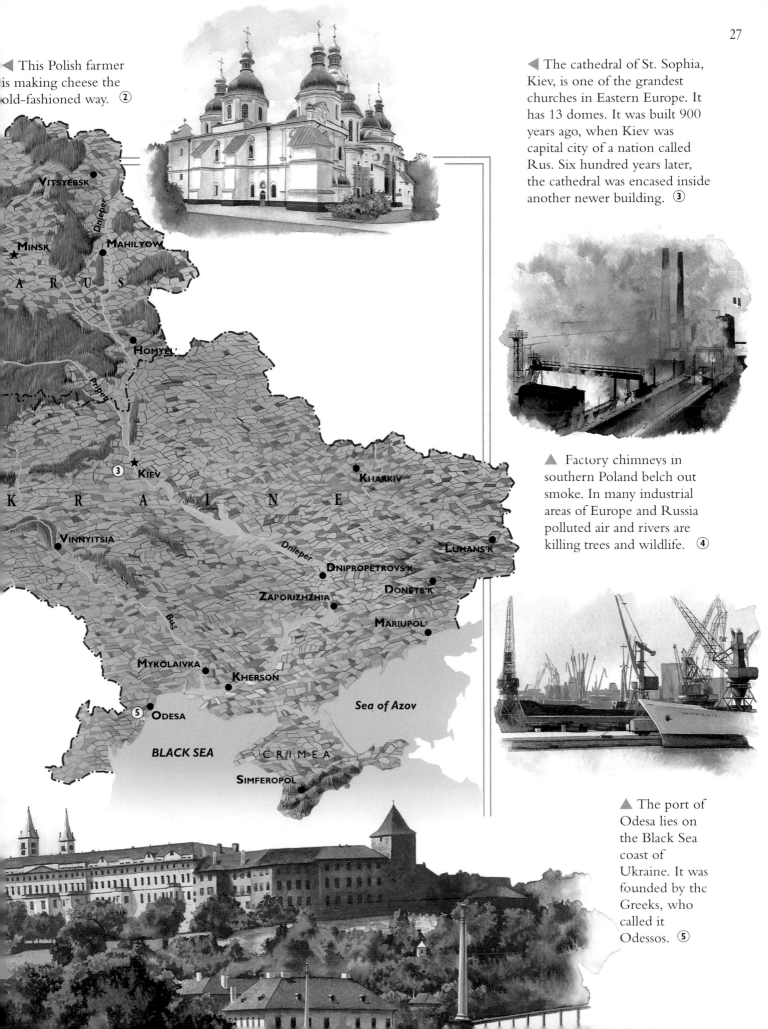

◄ This Polish farmer is making cheese the old-fashioned way. ②

◄ The cathedral of St. Sophia, Kiev, is one of the grandest churches in Eastern Europe. It has 13 domes. It was built 900 years ago, when Kiev was capital city of a nation called Rus. Six hundred years later, the cathedral was encased inside another newer building. ③

▲ Factory chimneys in southern Poland belch out smoke. In many industrial areas of Europe and Russia polluted air and rivers are killing trees and wildlife. ④

▲ The port of Odesa lies on the Black Sea coast of Ukraine. It was founded by the Greeks, who called it Odessos. ⑤

VITSYEBSK

MINSK

MAHILYOW

Dnieper

B A R U S

HOMYEL'

Pripeg

K R A I N E

③ KIEV

KHARKIV

VINNYITSIA

Dnieper

LUHANS'K

DNIPROPETROVS'K

ZAPORIZHZHIA

DONETS'K

Bug

MARIUPOL'

MYKOLAIVKA

KHERSON

Sea of Azov

⑤ ODESA

BLACK SEA

C R I M E A

SIMFEROPOL

THE BALKANS

THE southeastern corner of Europe is called the Balkans. The best farmland lies close to the Danube River in Serbia, Romania and Bulgaria. The broad valley of the Danube narrows to a small gap between the steep slopes of the Iron Gate gorge.

The Balkan nations are a dense patchwork of different peoples and different cultures.

▲ The Corinth Canal was cut through a narrow strip of land in Greece 100 years ago. Sea-going vessels are towed through by tugs. ⑦

▶ This is the Acropolis – a city of temples 2,500 years old. It was built on a hill overlooking Athens, now capital city of Greece. The most famous temple is the Parthenon, seen on the right. If you stood on the temple steps in the days of ancient Greece, you could look out for enemy ships approaching the coast. ⑥

◀ This is a farm building in Slovenia. Called a kozolec, it is used for drying and storing hay. ①

◀ A Romanian shepherd in from the Carpathian Mountains. ②

◀ Alexander Nevski Cathedral is in Bulgaria's capital, Sofia. It was completed soon after Bulgaria freed itself from Turkish rule, about 100 years ago. Nevski, a Russian prince who lived in the Middle Ages was much admired by all Slavs for his victories in battle. ③

▲ This is a whirling dervish, a Muslim worshipper from Konya in Turkey who performs a wild dance. ④

▼ People still live in these ancient cave-houses in Cappadocia, Turkey. ⑤

Scale
0   200 km

BLACK SEA

SAMSUN

ERZURUM

ANKARA ★

Kizilirmak

T U R K E Y

ESKIŞEHIR

L. Van

KAYSERI

⑤

L. Tuz

DIYARBAKIR

Tigris

④

KONYA

Euphrates

ADANA

GAZIANTEP

ANTALYA

CYPRUS

NICOSIA ★

TURKEY

MOST of the lands on this map (and on page 36) were once under Turkish rule. A small part of Europe around Istanbul still belongs to Turkey. Most of the country lies across the Bosporus strait in Asia. About half of all Turks still work in the fields, many on small hill farms with just a few sheep and goats.

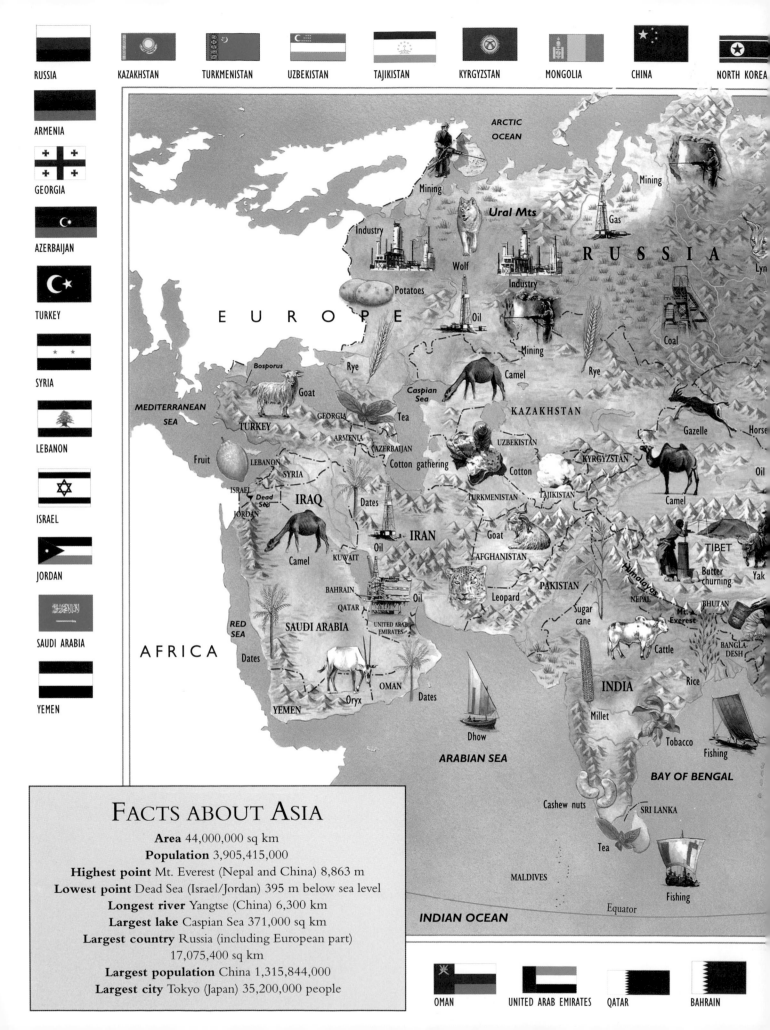

RUSSIA
KAZAKHSTAN
TURKMENISTAN
UZBEKISTAN
TAJIKISTAN
KYRGYZSTAN
MONGOLIA
CHINA
NORTH KOREA

ARMENIA
GEORGIA
AZERBAIJAN
TURKEY
SYRIA
LEBANON
ISRAEL
JORDAN
SAUDI ARABIA
YEMEN

OMAN
UNITED ARAB EMIRATES
QATAR
BAHRAIN

FACTS ABOUT ASIA

Area 44,000,000 sq km
Population 3,905,415,000
Highest point Mt. Everest (Nepal and China) 8,863 m
Lowest point Dead Sea (Israel/Jordan) 395 m below sea level
Longest river Yangtse (China) 6,300 km
Largest lake Caspian Sea 371,000 sq km
Largest country Russia (including European part)
17,075,400 sq km
Largest population China 1,315,844,000
Largest city Tokyo (Japan) 35,200,000 people

ARCTIC OCEAN
Mining
Ural Mts
Gas
Mining
R U S S I A
Industry
Wolf
Industry
Potatoes
Lyn
Oil
Mining
Coal
E U R O P E
Rye
Camel
Rye
Bosporus
Goat
Caspian Sea
KAZAKHSTAN
Gazelle
Horse
MEDITERRANEAN SEA
GEORGIA
Tea
TURKEY
ARMENIA
UZBEKISTAN
KYRGYZSTAN
Oil
AZERBAIJAN
Cotton gathering
Cotton
Camel
Fruit
LEBANON
TURKMENISTAN
TAJIKISTAN
ISRAEL
SYRIA
Dead Sea
IRAQ
Dates
IRAN
Goat
JORDAN
Oil
AFGHANISTAN
TIBET
Camel
KUWAIT
Butter churning
Yak
BAHRAIN
Leopard
PAKISTAN
QATAR
Oil
NEPAL
Mt. Everest
BHUTAN
RED SEA
SAUDI ARABIA
UNITED ARAB EMIRATES
Sugar cane
BANGLA-DESH
AFRICA
Cattle
Dates
Rice
OMAN
Dates
INDIA
YEMEN
Oryx
Tobacco
Millet
Fishing
Dhow
ARABIAN SEA
BAY OF BENGAL
Cashew nuts
SRI LANKA
Tea
MALDIVES
Fishing
Equator
INDIAN OCEAN

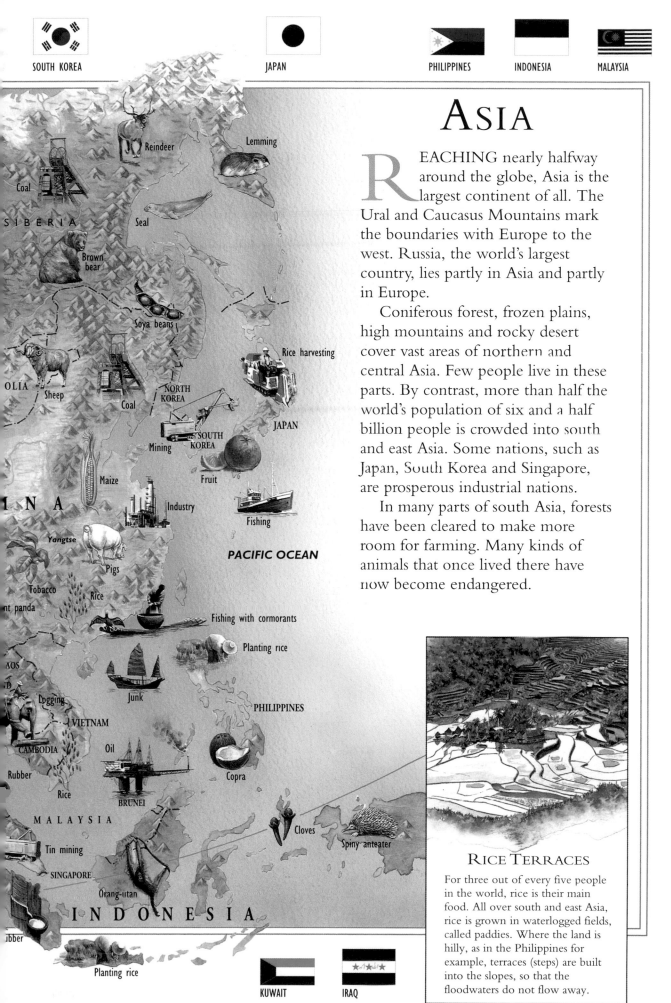

ASIA

REACHING nearly halfway around the globe, Asia is the largest continent of all. The Ural and Caucasus Mountains mark the boundaries with Europe to the west. Russia, the world's largest country, lies partly in Asia and partly in Europe.

Coniferous forest, frozen plains, high mountains and rocky desert cover vast areas of northern and central Asia. Few people live in these parts. By contrast, more than half the world's population of six and a half billion people is crowded into south and east Asia. Some nations, such as Japan, South Korea and Singapore, are prosperous industrial nations.

In many parts of south Asia, forests have been cleared to make more room for farming. Many kinds of animals that once lived there have now become endangered.

RICE TERRACES

For three out of every five people in the world, rice is their main food. All over south and east Asia, rice is grown in waterlogged fields, called paddies. Where the land is hilly, as in the Philippines for example, terraces (steps) are built into the slopes, so that the floodwaters do not flow away.

Map labels:

SOUTH KOREA
JAPAN
PHILIPPINES
INDONESIA
MALAYSIA
SINGAPORE

 SINGAPORE
 VIETNAM
 CAMBODIA
 LAOS
 THAILAND
 MYANMAR
 BANGLADESH
 BHUTAN
 NEPAL
 INDIA
 SRI LANKA
 MALDIVES
 PAKISTAN
 AFGHANISTAN
 IRAN

Reindeer
Lemming
Coal
SIBERIA
Seal
Brown bear
Soya beans
Rice harvesting
OLIA
Sheep
Coal
NORTH KOREA
Mining
SOUTH KOREA
JAPAN
Fruit
Fishing
CHINA
Maize
Industry
Yangtse
Pigs
PACIFIC OCEAN
Tobacco
Rice
int panda
Fishing with cormorants
Planting rice
Junk
PHILIPPINES
AOS
Logging
VIETNAM
CAMBODIA
Oil
Rubber
Rice
BRUNEI
Copra
Cloves
Spiny anteater
MALAYSIA
Tin mining
SINGAPORE
Orang-utan
INDONESIA
ibber
Planting rice

KUWAIT
IRAQ

NATIONS OF ASIA

AFGHANISTAN
Area 652,225 sq km **Population** 29,863,000
Capital Kabul **Languages** Pashto, Dari

ARMENIA
Area 29,800 sq km **Population** 3,016,000
Capital Yerevan **Language** Armenian

AZERBAIJAN
Area 88,600 sq km **Population** 8,411,000
Capital Baku **Language** Azeri

BAHRAIN
Area 691.2 sq km **Population** 727,000
Capital Manama **Language** Arabic

BANGLADESH
Area 143,998 sq km **Pop.** 141,822,000
Capital Dhaka **Languages** Bangla, English

BHUTAN
Area 47,000 sq km **Population** 2,163,000
Capital Thimphu **Language** Dzongkha

BRUNEI
Area 5,765 sq km **Population** 374,000
Capital Bandar Seri Begawan
Languages Malay, Chinese

▲ Indian girl ⑥

MYANMAR
Area 672,552 sq km **Population** 50,519,000
Capital Yangon **Language** Burmese

CAMBODIA
Area 181,035 sq km **Population** 14,071,000
Capital Phnom Penh **Language** Khmer

CHINA
Area 9,571,300 sq km **Population**
1,315,844,000 **Capital** Beijing
Language Chinese (many dialects)

EAST TIMOR
Area 14,874 sq km **Population** 947,000
Capital Dili **Languages** Tetum, Portuguese

GEORGIA
Area 69,700 sq km **Population** 4,474,000
Capital Tbilisi **Language** Georgian

INDIA
Area 3,287,590 sq km **Pop.** 1,103,371,000
Capital New Delhi **Languages** Hindi, Bangla,
Bihari, Telugu, Marathi, Tamil, English

INDONESIA
Area 1,904,569 sq km **Pop.** 222,781,000
Capital Jakarta **Language** Indonesian

IRAN
Area 1,648,000 sq km **Population** 69,515,000
Capital Tehran **Language** Farsi

IRAQ
Area 438,317 sq km **Population** 28,807,000
Capital Baghdad **Language** Arabic

ISRAEL
Area 21,946 sq km **Population** 6,725,000
Capital Jerusalem **Languages** Hebrew, Arabic

◀ Omani boy ①

KAZAKHSTAN
Area 2,717,300 sq km **Pop.** 14,825,000
Capital Astana **Languages** Kazakh, Russian

KUWAIT
Area 17,818 sq km **Population** 2,687,1000
Capital Kuwait **Language** Arabic

▶ Vietnamese boy ⑤

JAPAN
Area 377,815 sq km **Pop.** 128,085,000
Capital Tokyo **Language** Japanese

JORDAN
Area 97,740 sq km **Population** 5,703,000
Capital Amman **Language** Arabic

KYRGYZSTAN
Area 198,500 sq km **Population** 5,264,000
Capital Bishkek **Language** Kyrgyz

LAOS
Area 236,800 sq km **Population** 5,924,000
Capital Vientiane **Languages** Lao, French

LEBANON
Area 10,452 sq km Population 3,577,000
Capital Beirut Language Arabic

MALAYSIA
Area 329,758 sq km Pop. 25,347,000
Capital Kuala Lumpur Language Malay

NEPAL
Area 147,181 sq km Pop. 27,133,000
Capital Kathmandu Language Nepali

▲ Yakut girl from Russia ②

OMAN
Area 271,950 sq km Population 2,567,000
Capital Muscat Language Arabic

PAKISTAN
Area 803,943 sq km Pop. 157,935,000
Capital Islamabad Language Urdu

PHILIPPINES
Area 300,000 sq km Population 83,054,000
Capital Manila Languages English, Pilipino

QATAR
Area 11,437 sq km Population 813,000
Capital Doha Language Arabic

RUSSIA
Area 17,075,400 sq km Pop. 143,202,000
Capital Moscow Language Russian, 38 other languages

SAUDI ARABIA
Area 2,400,900 sq km Pop. 24,573,000
Capital Riyadh Language Arabic

SINGAPORE
Area 616 sq km Population 4,326,000
Languages Chinese, English, Malay, Tamil

SOUTH KOREA
Area 99,222 sq km Population 47,817,000
Capital Seoul Language Korean

SRI LANKA
Area 64,453 sq km Population 20,743,000
Capital Colombo Languages Sinhalese, Tamil

SYRIA
Area 185,180 sq km Population 19,043,000
Capital Damascus Language Arabic

TAJIKISTAN
Area 143,100 sq km Population 6,507,000
Capital Dushanbe Language Tajik

▼ Japanese boy ③

THAILAND
Area 513,115 sq km Population 64,233,000
Capital Bangkok Language Thai

TURKEY
Area 779,452 sq km Population 73,193,000
Capital Ankara Language Turkish

TURKMENISTAN
Area 488,100 sq km Population 4,833,000
Capital Ashkhabad Language Turkmen

UNITED ARAB EMIRATES
Area 75,150 sq km Population 4,496,000
Capital Abu Dhabi Language Arabic

UZBEKISTAN
Area 447,400 sq km Population 26,593,000
Capital Tashkent Language Uzbek

VIETNAM
Area 328,566 sq km Population 84,238,000
Capital Hanoi Languages Vietnamese, French

YEMEN
Area 477,530 sq km Population 20,975,000
Capital San'a Language Arabic

SIBERIA

YAKUTSK

SEA OF OKHOTSK

Sakhalin

Lena

IRKUTSK

L. Baikal

ULAN BATOR

MONGOLIA

ÜMQI

HARBIN

VLADIVOSTOK

SHENYANG

NORTH KOREA

PYONGYANG

SEOUL

SOUTH KOREA

BEIJING

TIANJIN

JAPAN

TOKYO

YOKOHAMA

KYOTO

OSAKA

KITAKYUSHU

Amur

Kuril Islands

Ryukyu Is.

LANZHOU

XI'AN

NANJING

SHANGHAI

CHINA

WUHAN

Huang

Yangtse

TIBET

CHONGQING

CHANGSHA

T'AIPEI

PACIFIC OCEAN

LHASA

GUANGZHOU

HONG KONG

MANDU

BHUTAN

DHARA

MANDALAY

HANOI

BANGLA-DESH

MYANMAR

LAOS

VIENTIANE

Hainan

MANILA

PHILIPPINES

YANGON

THAILAND

VIETNAM

SOUTH CHINA SEA

BENGAL

BANGKOK

CAMBODIA

Mekong

PNOMH PENH

HO CHI MINH CITY

DAVAO

Andaman Is.

BRUNEI

Irian Jaya

MALAYSIA

Borneo

KUALA LUMPUR

Sulawesi

SINGAPORE

Sumatra

INDONESIA

Timor EAST TIMOR

OCEAN

JAKARTA

Java

SURABAYA

MALDIVES
Area 298 sq km Population 329,000
Capital Malé Language Divehi

MONGOLIA
Area 1,565,000 sq km Population 2,646,000
Capital Ulan Bator Language Kalkha Mongol

▶ Balinese girl ④

NORTH KOREA
Area 120,538 sq km Population 22,488,000
Capital Pyongyang Language Korean

RUSSIA

THE LARGEST country in the world, Russia reaches all the way from Eastern Europe to within a few kilometres of Alaska in North America.

Most Russians live west of the Urals. To the east are the endless forests and wilderness of Siberia.

▲ This statue, "The Motherland", is almost as high as the Statue of Liberty. It stands in Volgograd. During World War II, when the city was known as Stalingrad, it was here that the Russian army defeated the German invasion force. ⑥

◀ A carpet-maker from Tajikistan. ①

▶ This church is made entirely out of wood. ②

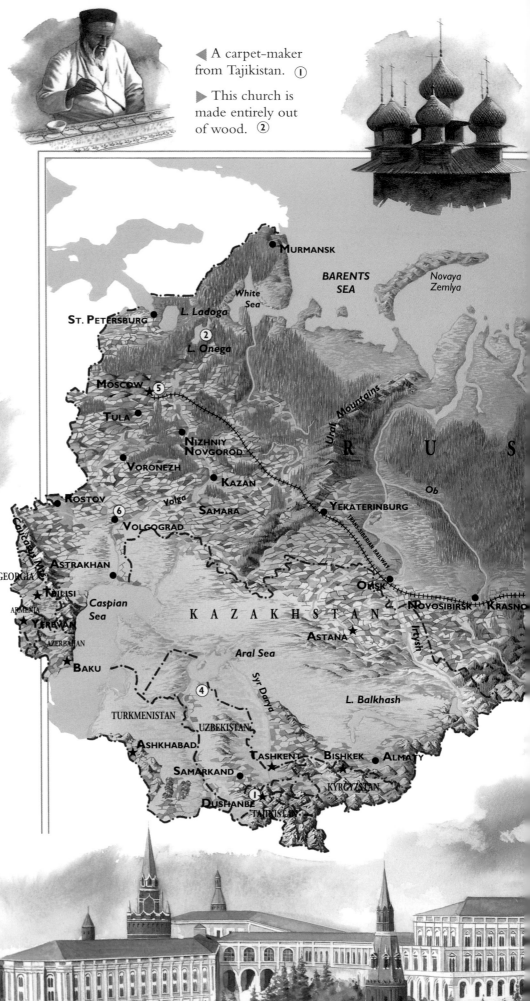

MURMANSK

BARENTS SEA

Novaya Zemlya

White Sea

L. Ladoga

ST. PETERSBURG

②

L. Onega

MOSCOW ⑤

TULA

NIZHNIY NOVGOROD

VORONEZH

KAZAN

Volga

ROSTOV

⑥

VOLGOGRAD

SAMARA

Ural Mountains

YEKATERINBURG

R U S

Ob

TRANS-SIBERIAN RAILWAY

OMSK

NOVOSIBIRSK

KRASNO

ASTRAKHAN

GEORGIA

TBILISI

ARMENIA

YEREVAN

AZERBAIJAN

Caspian Sea

K A Z A K H S T A N

ASTANA

Aral Sea

L. Balkhash

Irtysh

BAKU

TURKMENISTAN

④

Syr Darya

ASHKHABAD

UZBEKISTAN

TASHKENT

BISHKEK

ALMATY

SAMARKAND

KYRGYZSTAN

DUSHANBE ①

TAJIKISTAN

◀ A trip along the Trans-Siberian Railway is the longest rail journey you can make in the world. ③

▼ The Aral Sea, one of the world's largest lakes, is gradually drying up. In the past, two great rivers, the Syr Darya and the Amu Darya, flowed into it. Their waters have been used in the cotton fields, however, and the flow into the Aral Sea has been reduced to a trickle. Now fishing boats lie stranded on the dry lake bottom. ④

CENTRAL ASIA

THE LANDS to the east of the Caspian Sea are mostly desert. Mountains rise near the border with China. Five new nations occupy this region. Crops such as cotton, tobacco and cereals are grown near the rivers. The people who live in Central Asia are mostly Muslims.

ARCTIC OCEAN

Severnaya Zemlya

New Siberian Is.

NORVIK

Lena

Tunguska

S I B E R I A

YAKUTSK

MAGADAN

Kamchatka Peninsula

SEA OF OKHOTSK

Sakhalin

ngara

L. Baikal

③

Amur

KHABAROVSK

IRKUTSK

ULAN-UDE

VLADIVOSTOK

▼ At the heart of Moscow, Russia's capital city, lies the Kremlin. It was once a wooden fortress. ⑤

Scale
600 km

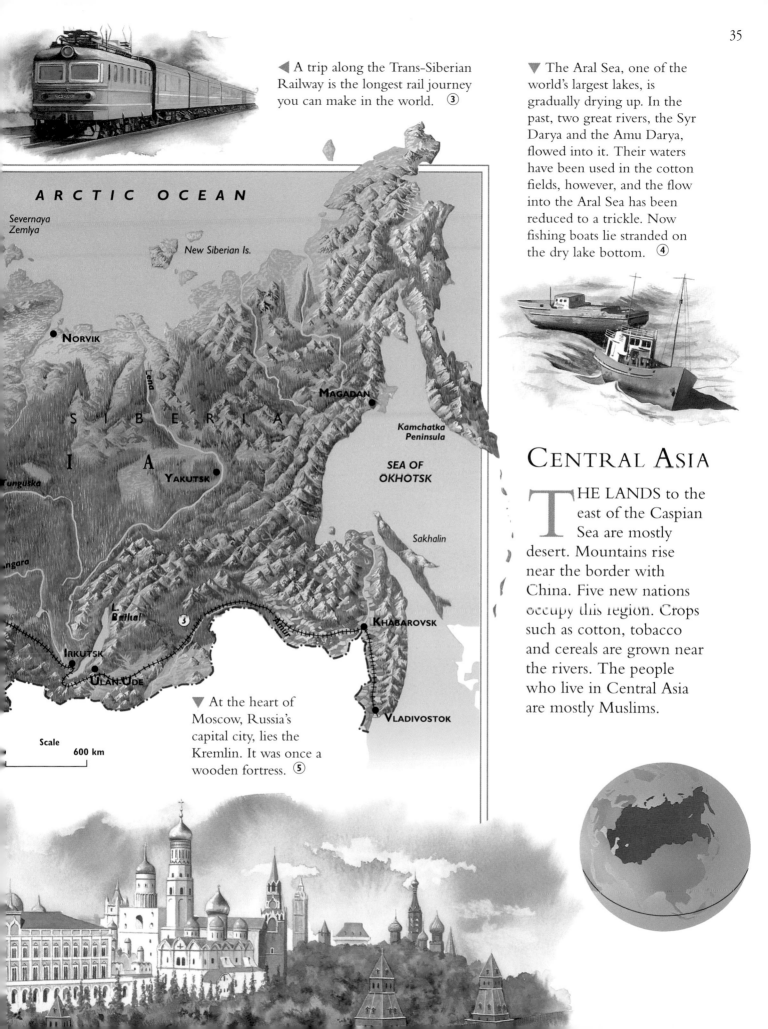

THE MIDDLE EAST

THE REGION that lies between Africa and South Asia is called the Middle East. It includes the Arabian peninsula, an L-shaped land lapped on three sides by the waters of the Red Sea, the Arabian Sea and the Persian Gulf. Nearly all of it is desert. One windblown part of it is completely uninhabited. It is called Rub al Khali, "The Empty Quarter".

Two great rivers, the Tigris and Euphrates, flow southeast to the Persian Gulf. Between them, almost an island, lies Mesopotamia. It was here, thousands of years ago, that people first learned to farm and where the first cities grew up.

▲ This is the entrance to the ancient city of Petra, Jordan. It was built into the cliffs by the Nabateans 2,000 years ago. ①

▼ A street seller in Jerusalem pours a glass of tamarindy, a fruit drink. ⑤

CASPIAN SEA

MASHHAD

BANDAR ABBAS

OMAN

KERMAN

DUBAI

Dasht-e Kavir

I   R   A   N

SHIRAZ

TEHRAN

ESFAHAN
③

PERSIAN GULF

QATAR

BAHRAIN
MANAMA

KERMANSHAH

②

ABADAN

KUWAIT

TABRIZ

L. Urmia

BAGHDAD

MESOPOTAMIA

BASRA

KUWAIT

K U R D I S T A N

Tigris

Euphrates

MOSUL

I   R   A   Q

An Nafud

ALEPPO

S Y R I A

DAMASCUS

AMMAN

JORDAN
①

LEBANON

BEIRUT

ISRAEL

JERUSALEM

TEL AVIV-YAFO

GAZA STRIP
⑤

R

▶ Oil is drilled from beneath the sea bed in the Persian Gulf using oil rigs like this. ②

ARABIAN SEA

N
O
M
A
N

S A U D I   A R A B I A

Rub al Khali

A

JIDDAH
MECCA

YEMEN
SAN'A ★
ADEN
MUKALLA

Scale
0 ━━━ 400 km

(above) This woman is a Kurd. Her people come from Kurdistan, a hilly land that includes parts of northern Iraq, north-western Iran and southeastern Turkey. ④

▲ The royal mosque in Esfahan, Iran, was built 400 years ago by an emperor called Shah Abbas. He ruled over a great empire in the Middle East. He made Esfahan, his capital, one of the largest and most beautiful cities in the world. Fifteen hundred metres above sea level on a dry, barren plain, more than one million people lived amongst the tree-lined avenues, parks and bustling bazaars. There were 162 mosques (places of Muslim worship) and 273 public baths! ③

SOUTH ASIA

NINETY of the world's hundred highest peaks are found in the Himalaya and Karakoram ranges. The Ganges and the Brahmaputra rivers flow down from the mountains. They meet and form a delta, a swampy tangle of river mouths, at the sea.

▲ Indian farmworkers take a ride on the roof of a train. It is the only way to travel when the train is packed full! India is criss-crossed by many railways. Most were built by the British, who once ruled India. ⑥

▼ If you were to stand on the roof-tops of Kathmandu, capital city of Nepal, this is what you would see. The Himalaya mountains tower all around. ⑤

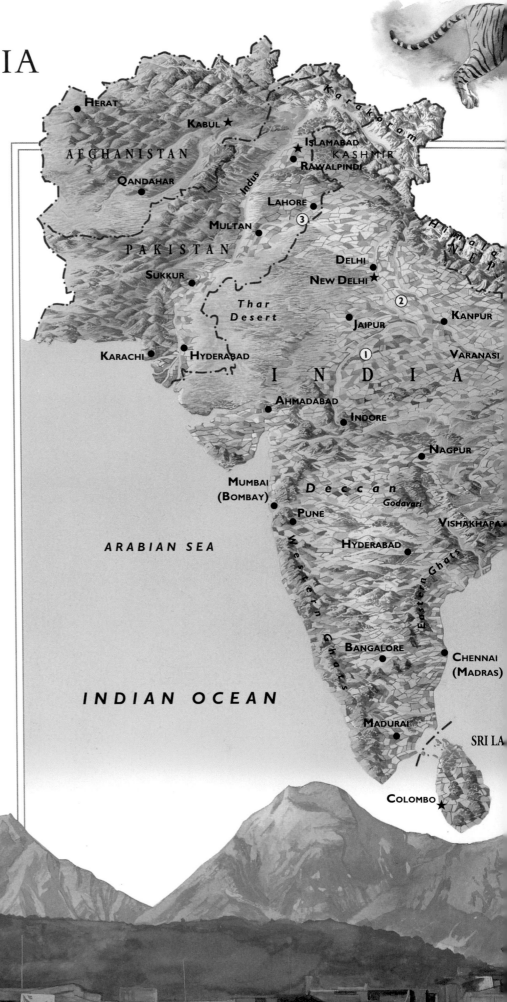

HERAT

KABUL ★

AFGHANISTAN

QANDAHAR

ISLAMABAD ★
KASHMIR
RAWALPINDI

Indus

LAHORE

③

MULTAN

PAKISTAN

DELHI

SUKKUR

NEW DELHI ★

Thar Desert

②

JAIPUR

KANPUR

KARACHI

HYDERABAD

①

VARANASI

I N D I A

AHMADABAD

INDORE

NAGPUR

MUMBAI (BOMBAY)

D e c c a n

Godavari

PUNE

VISHAKHAPA

ARABIAN SEA

HYDERABAD

Western Ghats

Eastern Ghats

BANGALORE

CHENNAI (MADRAS)

INDIAN OCEAN

MADURAI

SRI LA

COLOMBO ★

Karakoram

Himalaya

NEPAL

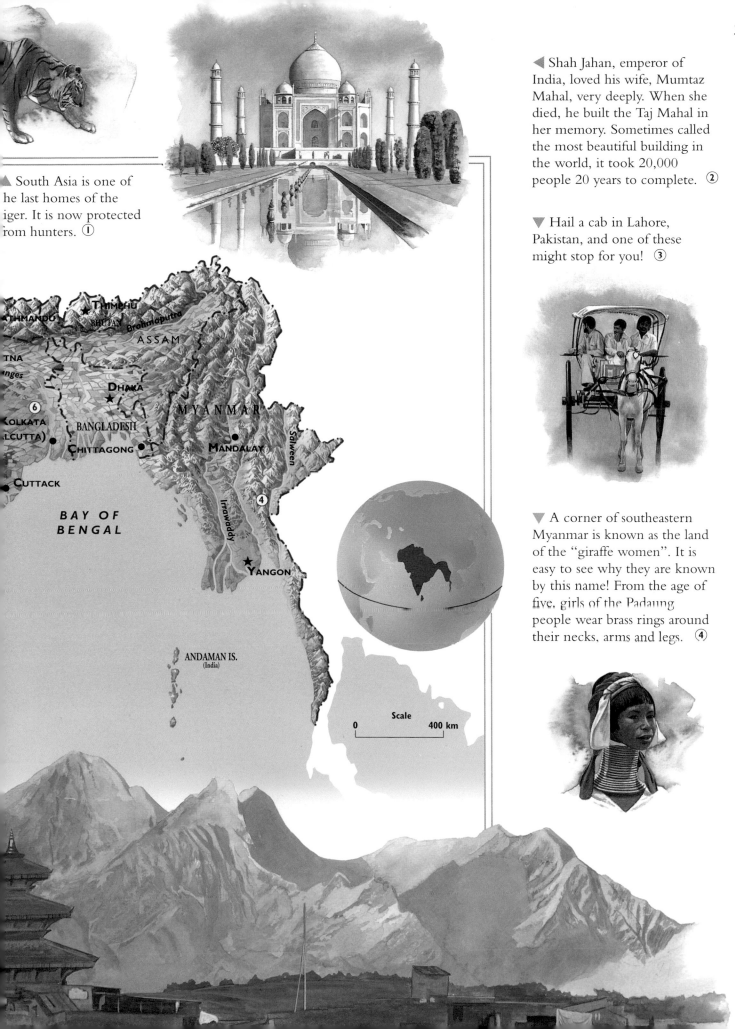

▲ South Asia is one of the last homes of the tiger. It is now protected from hunters. ①

◄ Shah Jahan, emperor of India, loved his wife, Mumtaz Mahal, very deeply. When she died, he built the Taj Mahal in her memory. Sometimes called the most beautiful building in the world, it took 20,000 people 20 years to complete. ②

▼ Hail a cab in Lahore, Pakistan, and one of these might stop for you! ③

▼ A corner of southeastern Myanmar is known as the land of the "giraffe women". It is easy to see why they are known by this name! From the age of five, girls of the Padaung people wear brass rings around their necks, arms and legs. ④

THIMPHU
BHUTAN
Brahmaputra
ASSAM
KATHMANDU
PATNA
Ganges
DHAKA
KOLKATA (CALCUTTA) ⑥
BANGLADESH
CHITTAGONG
MYANMAR
MANDALAY
Salween
CUTTACK
Irrawaddy
④
BAY OF BENGAL
YANGON
ANDAMAN IS. (India)

Scale
0   400 km

SOUTH-EAST ASIA

ALL the countries shown on this map have tropical climates. Most of the year it is very hot and there is a lot of rain. The valleys and plains are packed with rice fields, villages and towns.

Many different peoples live in Southeast Asia. Some forest peoples still lead traditional ways of life in Borneo and New Guinea.

▲ Children cross over a wooden bridge in southern Vietnam. This part of the country, near the mouth of the Mekong River, is flat and marshy with many rivers. Bridges have to be built on tall stilts to keep clear of floods. ⑦

▶ This is the great temple of Angkor Wat in Cambodia. Eight hundred years ago, a huge city of one million people surrounded this building. It was a very holy place where people came to worship. Now Angkor Wat stands in the middle of a jungle. Parts of it are crumbling away. ⑥

◀ This giant lizard lives on an Indonesian island. It is called the Komodo dragon. ①

◀ The island of Bali is famous for its dancers. The girls wear colourful traditional costumes. Their performances delight Bali's many visitors. ②

◀ This village in the Philippines is built in the sea. It is located off the southern tip of the island of Mindanao. The houses stand on stilts in a calm bay called a lagoon. The villagers get most of their food from the sea. Their fishing boats, called vintas, have brightly coloured sails. ③

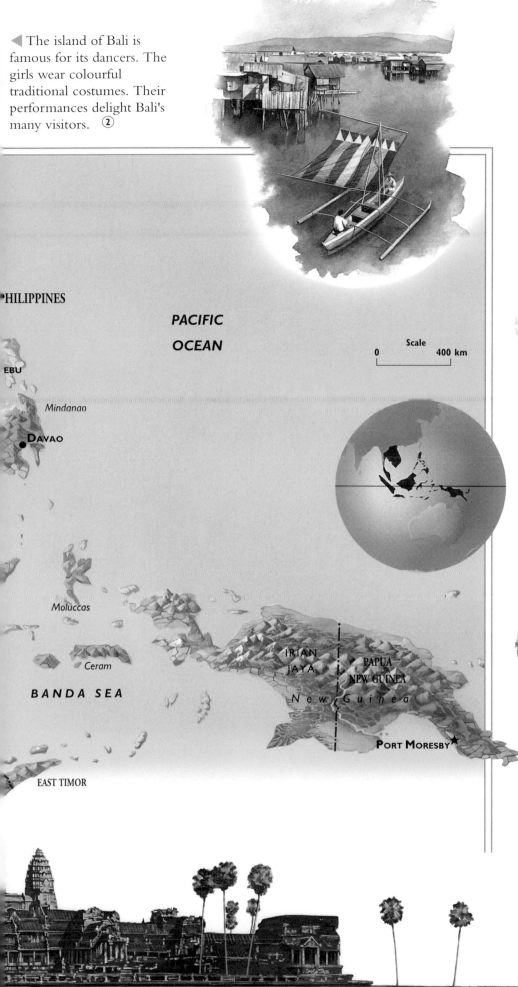

PHILIPPINES

PACIFIC OCEAN

Scale
0   400 km

EBU

Mindanao

● DAVAO

Moluccas

Ceram

BANDA SEA

IRIAN JAYA

PAPUA NEW GUINEA

New Guinea

PORT MORESBY ★

EAST TIMOR

▲ A man rides his ox-cart through the streets of a Malaysian town. This may soon be a scene of the past. Malaysia is fast becoming a prosperous industrial nation. Kuala Lumpur, the capital, is now a modern city. ④

▲ Many Indonesian islands are still covered with thick tropical rainforest—although the forests are being cut down at a rapid rate. More different kinds of plants and animals live here than in any other part of the world. This is an illustration of Rafflesia, the largest flower in the world. Measuring about 1 m across, it grows on the island of Sumatra. The petals smell like rotting meat! ⑤

CHINA

VERY FEW people live in western China, a land of high mountains and dry deserts. Eastern China could not be more different. It is home to more than a billion people, one fifth of the world's population. Two of the world's longest rivers flow across the landscape. They are the Huang He, or "Yellow River", after the colour of the soil in the surrounding countryside, and the Yangtse.

▲ This bronze statue of a horse is about 30 cm high and 1,800 years old. It was found at a place in central China close to where the Silk Road used to pass. This was an ancient trail that ran from China across Asia to the Middle East. ⑧

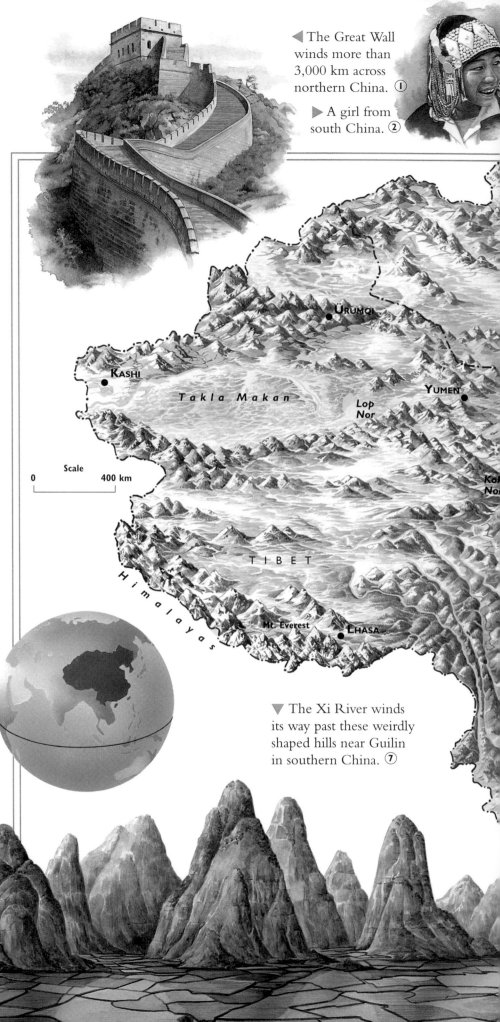

◀ The Great Wall winds more than 3,000 km across northern China. ①

▶ A girl from south China. ②

▼ The Xi River winds its way past these weirdly shaped hills near Guilin in southern China. ⑦

ÜRÜMQI
KASHI
Takla Makan
Lop Nor
YUMEN
TIBET
Himalayas
Mt. Everest
LHASA

Scale
0   400 km

◀ This farmer goes to market with his load of ducks and chickens. ③

◀ This round building in Beijing, China's capital city, is called the Temple of Heaven. It was built for an emperor nearly 500 years ago. He wished to pray to the gods for a good harvest each year. The temple has four main doors, one for each season. After the Temple was burnt down in a fire 100 years ago, 32 officials were beheaded. ④

▲ A funeral procession crosses the fields in South Korea. Although they are now the inhabitants of a modern industrial country, many people keep their traditional ways of life. Here, men and women are dressed in white, the Korean colour of mourning. The procession is led by people carrying banners. The dead man will be buried in a mound of earth. ⑤

▲ Hong Kong is a large, crowded, modern city. The centre of the city close to its famous harbour bristles with skyscrapers. Hong Kong was for many years a possession of Great Britain. It has now once again become part of China. ⑥

ULAN BATOR

GOLIA

B

HARBIN

SHENYANG

NORTH KOREA

PYONGYANG

① BEIJING ④

TIANJIN

SEOUL

⑤ SOUTH KOREA

TAIYUAN

JINAN

YELLOW SEA

QINGDAO

PUSAN

LANZHOU

Huang

XI'AN

ZHENGZHOU

Grand Canal

C H I N A

NANJING

SHANGHAI

CHENGDU ③

WUHAN

Yangtze

EAST CHINA SEA

ONGQING

CHANGSHA

T'AIPEI

⑦

GUANGZHOU

IMING

HONG KONG

MACAU ⑥

Hainan

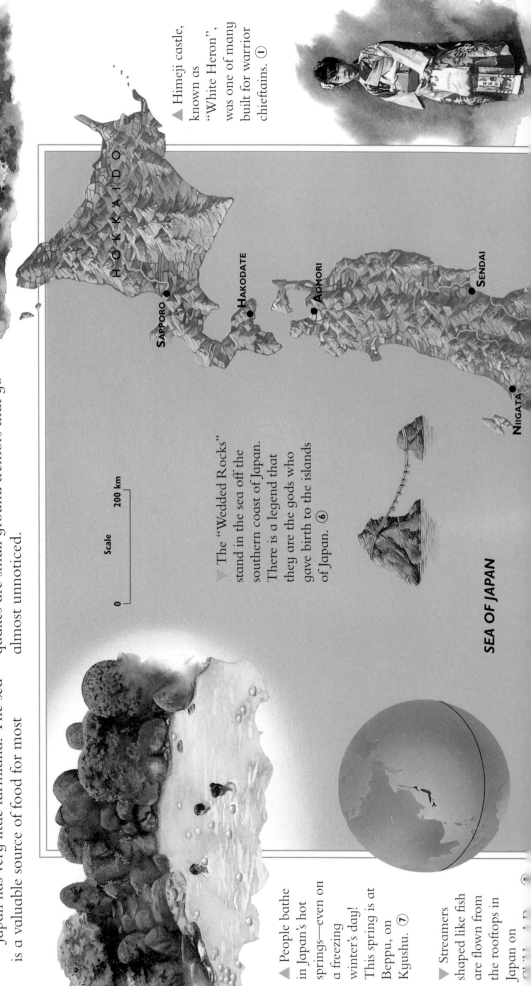

JAPAN

FOUR large islands, and quite a few small ones, make up the country of Japan. The main islands are, in order of size, Honshu, Hokkaido, Kyushu and Shikoku. Most of Japan is mountain and forest. The few plains and valleys are crammed with rice fields and cities.

Japan has very little farmland. The sea is a valuable source of food for most

Japanese. More fish is eaten in Japan than anywhere else in the world. The modern fishing fleet catches more fish than any other country.

Each year there are about 5,000 earthquakes. Japan would seem to be a dangerous place to live! In fact, most quakes are small ground tremors that go almost unnoticed.

▲ Himeji castle, known as "White Heron", was one of many built for warrior chieftains. ①

Scale

0   200 km

HOKKAIDO

● SAPPORO

● HAKODATE

● AOMORI

● SENDAI

● NIIGATA

▼ The "Wedded Rocks" stand in the sea off the southern coast of Japan. There is a legend that they are the gods who gave birth to the islands of Japan. ⑥

SEA OF JAPAN

▲ People bathe in Japan's hot springs—even on a freezing winter's day! This spring is at Beppu, on Kyushu. ⑦

▼ Streamers shaped like fish are flown from the rooftops in Japan on

平和日本

children aged seven, five and three attend a festival called *schichi-go-san.* ②

▲ The Japanese write using pictures, called characters, instead of our alphabet. This boy is learning to write well. ③

YOKOHAMA

② Tokyo ★

④

Mt Fuji

NAGOYA

N

KYOTO

⑥

OSAKA

③

WAKAYAMA

KOBE

O

① H

OKAYAMA

⑤

HIROSHIMA

TAKAMATSU

MATSAYUMA

SHIKOKU

PACIFIC OCEAN

KITAKYUSHU

⑦

KYUSHU

FUKUOKA

NAGASAKI

MIYAZAKI

▼ A high-speed train, named the "bullet train" after the shape of its nose, whistles past Mount Fuji. ④

Ryukyu Islands

Okinawa

NATIONS OF OCEANIA

AUSTRALIA
Area 7,682,300 sq km **Population** 20,155,000
Capital Canberra **Language** English

FIJI
Area 18,376 sq km **Population** 848,000
Capital Suva **Languages** Fijian, Hindi, English

KIRIBATI
Area 811 sq km **Population** 99,000
Capital Tarawa **Languages** I-Kiribati, English

NAURU
Area 21 sq km **Pop.** 14,000 **Capital** Yaren
District **Languages** Nauruan, English

▲ Australian boy ③

NEW ZEALAND
Area 270,534 sq km **Population** 4,028,000
Capital Wellington **Languages** English, Maori

PAPUA NEW GUINEA
Area 462,840 sq km **Population** 5,887,000
Capital Port Moresby **Languages** Pidgin,
English, Motu

SAMOA
Area 2,831 sq km **Population** 185,000
Capital Apia **Languages** Samoan, English

◀ Boy from Solomon Islands ①

INDIAN OCEAN

NORTHERN TERRITORY

Diamonds
Cattle
Emu
Boab tree
Termite mound
Frilled
WESTERN AUSTRALIA
Mining
A U S
Manta ray
Wallaby
Wheat
Road train
Sheep
Sailing
Whale shark

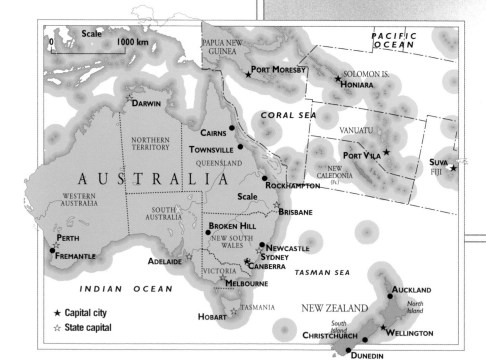

Scale
0   1000 km

PAPUA NEW GUINEA
PORT MORESBY
SOLOMON IS.
HONIARA
PACIFIC OCEAN
DARWIN
CORAL SEA
CAIRNS
TOWNSVILLE
VANUATU
QUEENSLAND
PORT VILA
NEW CALEDONIA (Fr.)
SUVA FIJI
NORTHERN TERRITORY
AUSTRALIA
ROCKHAMPTON
Scale
WESTERN AUSTRALIA
SOUTH AUSTRALIA
BRISBANE
BROKEN HILL
NEW SOUTH WALES
PERTH
NEWCASTLE
FREMANTLE
SYDNEY
CANBERRA
ADELAIDE
VICTORIA
TASMAN SEA
MELBOURNE
INDIAN OCEAN
AUCKLAND
TASMANIA
NEW ZEALAND
North Island
HOBART
South Island
★ Capital city
☆ State capital
WELLINGTON
CHRISTCHURCH
DUNEDIN

▲ Maori girl from New Zealand ②

SOLOMON ISLANDS
Area 27,556 sq km **Population** 478,000
Capital Honiara **Languages** English, Pidgin

TONGA
Area 748 sq km **Population** 102,000 **Capital**
Nuku'alofa **Languages** Tongan, English

AUSTRALIA   PAPUA NEW GUINEA   NAURU

KIRIBATI

SOLOMON ISLANDS

VANUATU

TUVALU

FIJI

SAMOA

TONGA

NEW ZEALAND

OCEANIA

OCEANIA is the name given to the group of countries located in the South Pacific Ocean. It is made up of Australia (itself an island continent), New Zealand, Papua New Guinea and the islands of the Pacific Ocean. (For a complete map of the Pacific islands see pages 6-7).

Human beings probably first arrived in Australia more than 50,000 years ago. Perhaps the first peoples to travel by sea, they came from Southeast Asia. Thousands of years later, people reached the Pacific Islands and New Zealand in their sturdy ocean-going canoes.

Ore train

Doctor

Saltwater crocodile

Great Barrier Reef

Snorkelling

Spiny anteater

Mining

QUEENSLAND

Sugar cane

Spinifex grass

Kangaroo

Cattle

Koala

L. Eyre

Darling

SOUTH AUSTRALIA

Mining

Shepherd

Wheat

NEW SOUTH WALES

Coal

Grapes

Murray

Sheep

VICTORIA

Grapes

Gas tanker

Duck-billed platypus

TASMANIA

Sperm whale

TASMAN SEA

Cattle

Kiwi

NEW ZEALAND

Sheep

Kakapo

Sheep

FACTS ABOUT OCEANIA

Area 8,923,000 sq km
Population 33,056,000
Highest point Mt. Wilhelm (Papua New Guinea) 4,509 m
Lowest point Lake Eyre (Australia) 16 m below sea level
Longest river Murray-Darling (Australia) 3,750 km
Largest lake Lake Eyre (Australia) 9,500 sq km
Largest country Australia 7,682,300 sq km
Largest population Australia 20,155,000
Largest city Sydney (Australia) 4,300,000 people

TUVALU
Area 26 sq km **Population** 10,000 **Capital** Funafuti **Languages** Tuvaluan, English
VANUATU
Area 12,190 sq km **Pop.** 211,000 **Capital** Port Vila **Languages** Bislama, English, French

AUSTRALIA

AUSTRALIA is about the same in area as the USA (excluding Alaska). Its population is only a tiny fraction of that country's. Much of the land in the west, covered by grass and low bushes, is dry scrub, known as the "bush". Most people live in the southeast.

▲ Sydney is Australia's largest city. It is situated on the south–eastern coast, where most Australian cities have grown up. Sydney is famous for two magnificent landmarks: the Opera House and Harbour Bridge. The roof of the Opera House was built to look like the sails of yachts on the harbour waters. The bridge, which carries both trains and cars, is known to local people as the "Coathanger"! **7**

◄ This Aborigine performs a traditional dance. Aborigines have lived in Australia for thousands of years. **1**

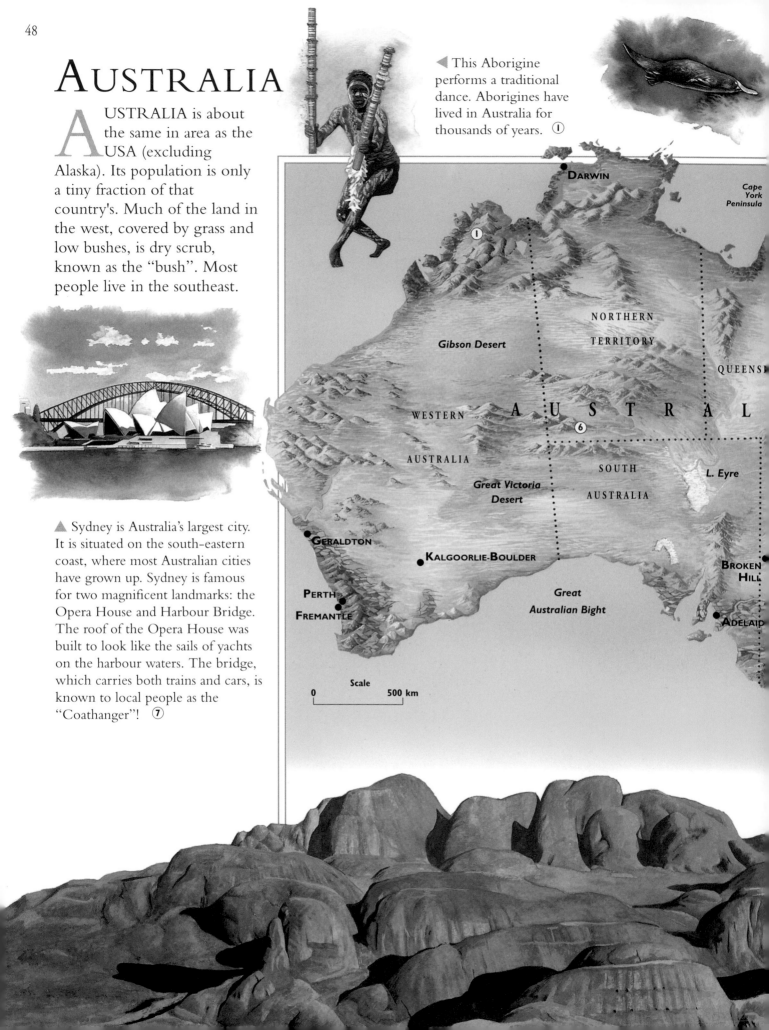

DARWIN

Cape York Peninsula

1

NORTHERN

TERRITORY

QUEENSI

Gibson Desert

WESTERN   A U S T R A L

6

AUSTRALIA

SOUTH

Great Victoria   AUSTRALIA   L. Eyre
Desert

GERALDTON

KALGOORLIE-BOULDER

BROKEN
HILL

PERTH
FREMANTLE

Great
Australian Bight

ADELAID

Scale

0   500 km

◄ The duckbilled platypus is a mammal, although it has webbed feet and a bill like a duck's. It even lays eggs! ②

SOLOMON ISLANDS ③

PACIFIC OCEAN

CORAL SEA

CAIRNS

Great Barrier Reef

Great Dividing Range

2

VANUATU

ROCKHAMPTON

NEW CALEDONIA (France)

BRISBANE

TASMAN SEA

Darling

W SOUTH WALES

NEWCASTLE
7 SYDNEY
CANBERRA

▼ The takahe, a rare flightless bird from New Zealand. ⑤

LBOURNE

TASMANIA

AUCKLAND
NORTH ISLAND
④

HOBART

NEW ZEALAND

SOUTH ISLAND

WELLINGTON

CHRISTCHURCH

Southern Alps

5

DUNEDIN
Stewart I.

◄ The Olgas mountains, like nearby Uluru (Ayers Rock), are sacred to the Aborigines. ⑥

◄ This house is built on stilts in the waters of a lagoon, a shallow bay. Some villages in the Solomon Islands cluster together on man-made islands built hundreds of years ago.

Like many Pacific islands, the Solomon Islands were first inhabited by people who sailed there from Southeast Asia. Today the islanders make a living from fishing, mining, palm oil and tourism. ③

FIJI
SUVA

▲ Geysers, gushing jets of hot water, are found in New Zealand. ④

NEW ZEALAND

NEW ZEALAND is made up of the North and South Islands. Both islands are mountainous. Grassy low-lands on South Island are grazed by sheep. Strange animals like the kiwi, a flightless bird, and the tuatara, a reptile left over from the Age of Dinosaurs, live only in New Zealand.

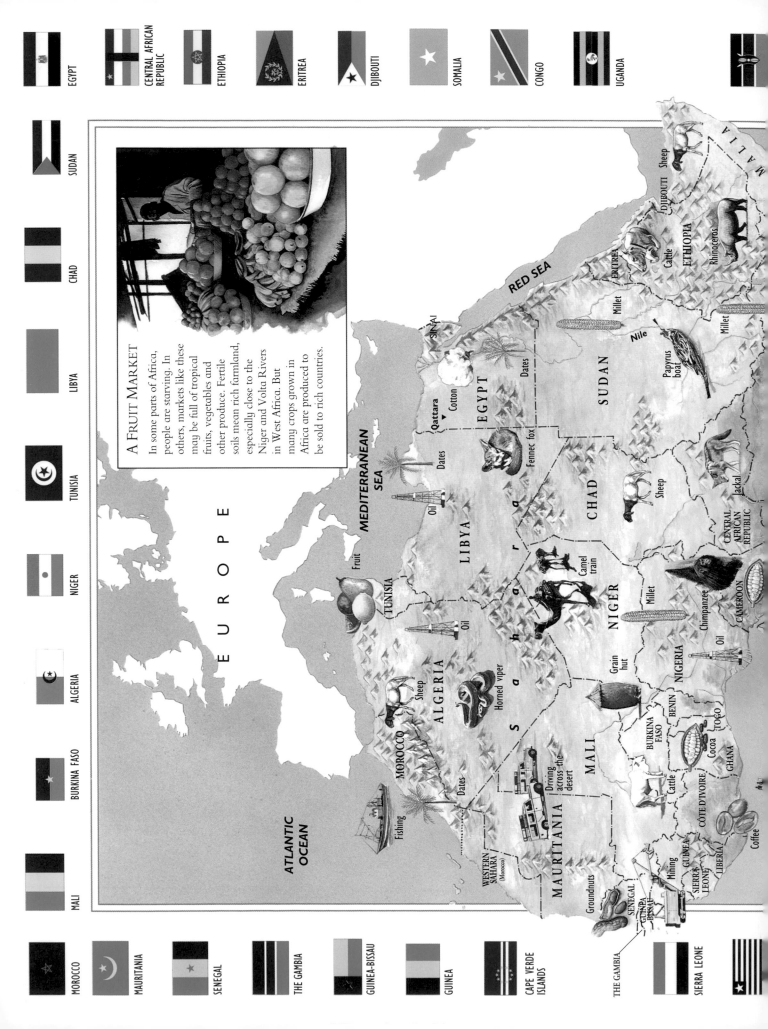

EGYPT

CENTRAL AFRICAN REPUBLIC

ETHIOPIA

ERITREA

DJIBOUTI

SOMALIA

CONGO

UGANDA

SUDAN

CHAD

LIBYA

TUNISIA

NIGER

ALGERIA

BURKINA FASO

MALI

MOROCCO

MAURITANIA

SENEGAL

THE GAMBIA

GUINEA-BISSAU

GUINEA

CAPE VERDE ISLANDS

THE GAMBIA

SIERRA LEONE

A FRUIT MARKET

In some parts of Africa, people are starving. In others, markets like these may be full of tropical fruits, vegetables and other produce. Fertile soils mean rich farmland, especially close to the Niger and Volta Rivers in West Africa. But many crops grown in Africa are produced to be sold to rich countries.

ATLANTIC OCEAN

EUROPE

MEDITERRANEAN SEA

RED SEA

SINAI

EGYPT

Qattara

Cotton

Dates

Nile

Papyrus boat

Fennec fox

SUDAN

Sheep

CHAD

Millet

ETHIOPIA

Sheep

Rhinoceros

Cattle

DJIBOUTI

Millet

Jackal

MOROCCO

Dates

Fruit

Oil

TUNISIA

Oil

LIBYA

Sahara

Camel train

Millet

NIGER

Grain hut

Oil

NIGERIA

CAMEROON

Chimpanzee

CENTRAL AFRICAN REPUBLIC

Sheep

Horned viper

ALGERIA

Fishing

Dates

Driving across the desert

WESTERN SAHARA (Morocco)

MAURITANIA

MALI

BURKINA FASO

BENIN

TOGO

Cocoa

GHANA

CÔTE D'IVOIRE

Cattle

Coffee

Groundnuts

SENEGAL

GUINEA-BISSAU

Mining

GUINEA

SIERRA LEONE

LIBERIA

AFRICA

AFRICA is surrounded by sea, except where it meets Asia at the Sinai peninsula. The second largest continent after Asia, it is a land of vast deserts, thick rainforests, rugged mountain chains and rolling grasslands.

Finds of prehistoric bones, footprints and carved stones lead scientists to think that humans originally came from Africa. It is believed these human ancestors hunted animals for food and learned to use tools on the grasslands of East Africa.

Hundreds of different peoples live all over Africa today. Often, many peoples share the same country. Islam is the religion of the north, while both traditional beliefs and Christianity are followed elsewhere. One hundred years ago, European countries like Britain, France, Germany and Portugal ruled over large parts of the continent. Today, all African countries are independent.

FACTS ABOUT AFRICA

Area 29,800,000 sq km
Population 905,936,000
Highest point Kilimanjaro (Tanzania) 5,894 m
Lowest point Qattara Depression (Egypt) 132 m below sea level
Longest river Nile 6,670 km
Largest lake Victoria 69,500 sq km
Largest country Sudan 2,505,813 sq km
Largest population Nigeria 131,530,000
Largest city Cairo (Egypt) 11,100,000 people

INDIAN OCEAN

MADAGASCAR
Chameleon

COMOROS
Dhow
Cashew nuts

Masai herdsman
Zebra
Hippopotamus
TANZANIA
BURUNDI
Gorilla
Lion
Hornbill
ANGOLA
Diamonds
Copper mine
ZAMBIA
Elephant
Tea
Tobacco
MALAWI
MOZAMBIQUE
ZIMBABWE
Impala
BOTSWANA
Diamonds
Mining
Mining
SWAZILAND
LESOTHO
Sheep
Ostrich
NAMIBIA
SOUTH AFRICA

RWANDA

BURUNDI

TANZANIA

MALAWI

MOZAMBIQUE

SEYCHELLES

COMOROS

MAURITIUS

SOUTH AFRICA

MADAGASCAR

SWAZILAND

LESOTHO

ZIMBABWE

ZAMBIA

BOTSWANA

NAMIBIA

CÔTE D'IVOIRE

GHANA

TOGO

BENIN

NIGERIA

CAMEROON

EQUATORIAL GUINEA

SÃO TOMÉ & PRÍNCIPE

GABON

CONGO-BRAZZAVILLE

ANGOLA

NATIONS OF AFRICA

▲ Wodaabe girl from Niger ①

ALGERIA
Area 2,381,741 sq km **Population** 32,854,000 **Capital** Algiers **Languages** Arabic, French

ANGOLA
Area 1,246,700 sq km **Population** 15,941,000 **Capital** Luanda **Languages** Portuguese, Bantu languages

BENIN
Area 112,622 sq km **Population** 8,439,000 **Capital** Porto-Novo **Language** French

BOTSWANA
Area 582,000 sq km **Population** 1,765,000 **Capital** Gaborone **Languages** English, Tswana

BURKINA FASO
Area 274,200 sq km **Population** 13,228,000 **Capital** Ouagadougou **Languages** French, Mossi

BURUNDI
Area 27,834 sq km **Population** 7,548,000 **Capital** Bujumbura **Languages** French, Kirundi, Swahili

CAMEROON
Area 475,442 sq km **Population** 16,322,000 **Capital** Yaoundé **Languages** French, English

CAPE VERDE ISLANDS
Area 4,033 sq km **Population** 507,000 **Capital** Praia **Languages** Portuguese, Crioulo

CENTRAL AFRICAN REPUBLIC
Area 622,984 sq km **Population** 4,038,000 **Capital** Bangui **Languages** French, Sango

CHAD
Area 1,284,000 sq km **Population** 9,749,000 **Capital** N'Djamena **Languages** French, Arabic

CONGO–BRAZZAVILLE
Area 342,000 sq km **Population** 3,999,000 **Capital** Brazzaville **Language** French

CÔTE D'IVOIRE
Area 322,462 sq km **Population** 18,154,000 **Capitals** Yamoussoukro, Abidjan **Languages** French, Malinke

DJIBOUTI
Area 23,200 sq km **Population** 793,000 **Capital** Djibouti **Languages** Arabic, French

EGYPT
Area 997,739 sq km **Pop.** 74,033,000 **Capital** Cairo **Language** Arabic

EQUATORIAL GUINEA
Area 28,051 sq km **Pop.** 504,000 **Capital** Malabo **Language** Spanish

ERITREA
Area 121,144 sq km **Pop.** 4,401,000 **Capital** Asmera **Language** Tigrinya

CONGO (Democratic Republic of)
Area 2,344,885 sq km **Population** 57,549,000 **Capital** Kinshasa **Languages** Swahili, Lingala, French

▲ Berber girl ⑥

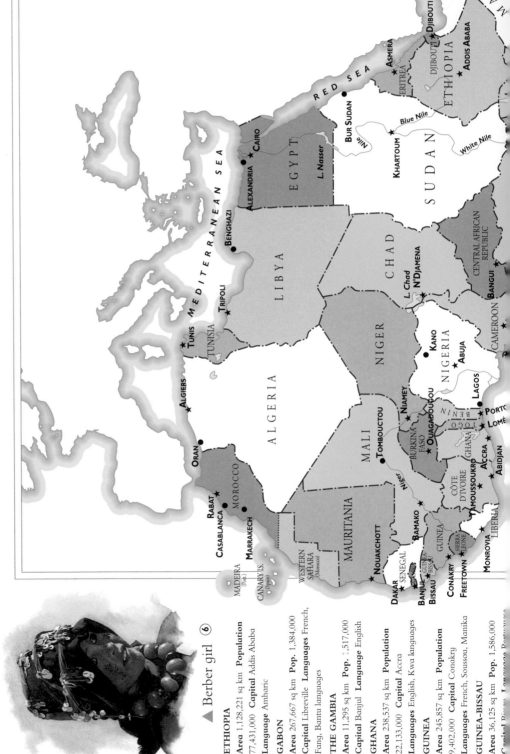

ETHIOPIA
Area 1,128,221 sq km **Population** 77,431,000 **Capital** Addis Ababa **Language** Amharic

GABON
Area 267,667 sq km **Pop.** 1,384,000 **Capital** Libreville **Languages** French, Fang, Bantu languages

THE GAMBIA
Area 11,295 sq km **Pop.** 1,517,000 **Capital** Banjul **Language** English

GHANA
Area 238,537 sq km **Population** 22,133,000 **Capital** Accra **Languages** English, Kwa languages

GUINEA
Area 245,857 sq km **Population** 9,402,000 **Capital** Conakry **Languages** French, Soussou, Manika

GUINEA-BISSAU
Area 36,125 sq km **Pop.** 1,586,000

Masai girl ②

MOZAMBIQUE
Area 799,380 sq km Population 19,792,000 Capital Maputo Languages Portuguese, Ronga, Shangaan, Muchope

NAMIBIA
Area 824,292 sq km Population 2,031,000 Capital Windhoek Languages English, Afrikaans, German

NIGER
Area 1,267,000 sq km Population 13,957,000 Capital Niamey Languages French, Hausa, Tuareg, Djerma, Fulani

NIGERIA
Area 923,768 sq km Population 131,530,000 Capital Abuja Languages English, Hausa, Yoruba, Ibo

RÉUNION
Area 2,512 sq km Population 785,000 Capital Saint-Denis Language French

Efe (pygmy) girl ③

UGANDA
Area 241,139 sq km Pop. 28,816,000 Capital Kampala Languages English, Luganda

WESTERN SAHARA
Area 266,000 sq km Pop. 341,000 Capital El Aaiun Language Arabic

ZAMBIA
Area 752,614 sq km Population 11,668,000 Capital Lusaka Languages English, Lozi

ZIMBABWE
Area 390,759 sq km Population 13,010,000 Capital Harare Languages English, Shona, Ndebele

Map

COMOROS · MADAGASCAR · ANTANANARIVO ★ · INDIAN OCEAN
MOMBASA · DAR ES SALAAM · BUJUMBURA · DODOMA ★ · TANZANIA · L. Nyasa · LILONGWE ★ · MALAWI · Zambezi · BEIRA · MOZAMBIQUE · ZIMBABWE · HARARE ★ · BULAWAYO · ZAMBIA · LUSAKA ★ · LUBUMBASHI · CONGO · KNSHASA ★ · ANGOLA · HUAMBO · LUANDA · CABINDA (Angola) · BOTSWANA · GABORONE ★ · NAMIBIA · WINDHOEK ★ · MAPUTO · SWAZILAND · PRETORIA ★ · JOHANNESBURG · MBABANE ★ · MASERU ★ · LESOTHO · SOUTH AFRICA · Orange · DURBAN · PORT ELIZABETH · CAPE TOWN
ATLANTIC OCEAN
Scale 0 — 1000 km · ★ Capital city

Nigerian boy ⑤

Zulu boy from South Africa ④

RWANDA
Area 26,338 sq km Population 9,038,000 Capital Kigali Languages French, Kinyarwanda, Swahili

SÃO TOMÉ AND PRÍNCIPE
Area 964 sq km Pop. 157,000 Capital São Tomé Language Portuguese

SENEGAL
Area 196,192 sq km Pop. 11,658,000 Capital Dakar Language French

SEYCHELLES
Area 454 sq km Pop. 81,000 Capital Victoria Languages English, Creole

SIERRA LEONE
Area 71,740 sq km Population 5,525,000 Capital Freetown Languages English, Krio, Mende, Limba, Temne

SOMALIA
Area 637,657 sq km Population 8,228,000 Capital Mogadishu Languages Somali, Arabic, English, Italian

SOUTH AFRICA
Area 1,221,037 sq km Population 47,432,000 Capitals Pretoria, Cape Town Languages Afrikaans, English, Xhosa, Zulu, Sesotho

SUDAN
Area 2,505,813 sq km Population 36,233,000 Capital Khartoum Languages Arabic, English

SWAZILAND
Area 17,363 sq km Pop. 1,032,000 Capital Mbabane Languages English, siSwati

TANZANIA
Area 945,087 sq km Population 38,329,000 Capital Dodoma Languages Swahili, English

TOGO
Area 56,785 sq km Population 6,145,000 Capital Lomé Languages French, Kabiye, Ewe

TUNISIA
Area 164,150 sq km Population 10,102,000 Capital Tunis Languages Arabic, Berber, French

KENYA
Area 580,367 sq km Pop. 34,256,000 Capital Nairobi Languages Swahili, English, Kikuyu, Luo

LESOTHO
Area 30,355 sq km Population 1,795,000 Capital Maseru Languages English, Sesotho

LIBERIA
Area 97,754 sq km Pop. 3,283,000 Capital Monrovia Language English

LIBYA
Area 1,775,500 sq km Pop. 5,853,000 Capital Tripoli Language Arabic

MADAGASCAR
Area 587,041 sq km Population 18,606,000 Capital Antananarivo Languages Malagasy, French

MALAWI
Area 118,484 sq km Population 12,884,000 Capital Lilongwe Languages English, Chichewa

MALI
Area 1,240,192 sq km Pop. 13,518,000 Capital Bamako Language French

MAURITANIA
Area 1,030,700 sq km Pop. 3,069,000 Capital Nouakchott Languages Arabic, Poular, Wolof, Solinke

MAURITIUS
Area 2,040 sq km Population 1,245,000 Capital Port Louis Languages English, Creole

MOROCCO
Area 446,550 sq km Population 31,478,000 Capital Rabat Languages Arabic, Berber, Spanish, French

NORTHERN AFRICA

A LARGE part of this map shows an area where hardly anybody lives. All the year round the Sahara Desert is hot and dry. Nothing grows in the bare, stony ground. Only a few parts of the Sahara are sandy. Some areas are quite mountainous.

Farmland and pastures lie to the south of the Sahara. This area, called the Sahel, is sometimes almost as dry as a desert. Crops cannot grow and grazing animals die.

◀ Morocco is famous for its colourful marketplaces, known as "souks". ①

▲ The people of West Africa dress up in style for special occasions! This man is wearing a hat made of parrot feathers and an elephant mask (note the large ears and long trunk). He wears this costume to show how wealthy and powerful he is. ⑦

ALGIERS
TUNIS
TUNISIA
RABAT
MOROCCO
CASABLANCA
MADEIRA (Portugal)
MARRAKECH
Atlas Mountains
ALGERIA
CANARY IS. (Spain)
LAS PALMAS
WESTERN SAHARA (Morocco)
SAHARA
Ahaggar
MAURITANIA
MALI
NOUAKCHOTT
TOMBOUCTOU
NIGER
Niger
L. Chad
SENEGAL
DAKAR
NIAMEY
THE GAMBIA
BAMAKO
OUAGADOUGOU
②
KANO
N'DJAMENA
GUINEA-BISSAU
BURKINA FASO
NIGERIA
GUINEA
④
BENIN
CONAKRY
ABUJA
Benue
SIERRA LEONE
CÔTE D'IVOIRE
L. Volta
GHANA
TOGO
FREETOWN
IBADAN
⑦
YAMOUSSOUKRO
LOMÉ
LAGOS
LIBERIA
ACCRA
CAMEROON
MONROVIA
ABIDJAN
DOUALA
YAOUNDÉ
GULF OF GUINEA
EQUATORIAL GUINEA
SÃO TOMÉ AND PRÍNCIPE

Scale
0   400 km

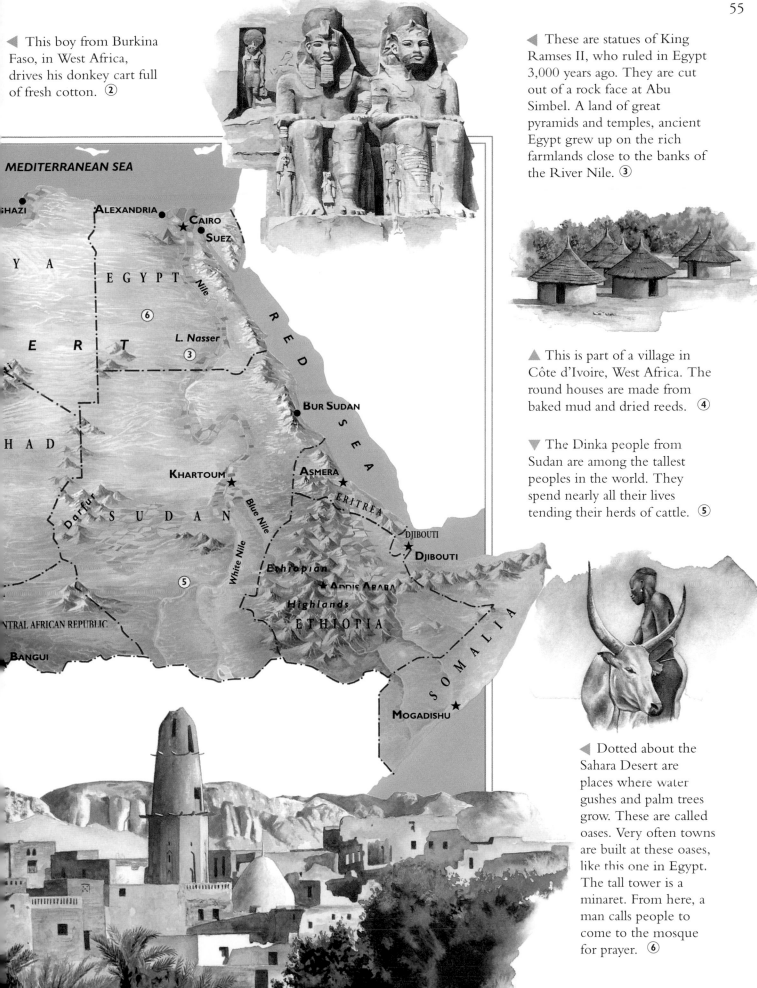

◄ This boy from Burkina Faso, in West Africa, drives his donkey cart full of fresh cotton. ②

◄ These are statues of King Ramses II, who ruled in Egypt 3,000 years ago. They are cut out of a rock face at Abu Simbel. A land of great pyramids and temples, ancient Egypt grew up on the rich farmlands close to the banks of the River Nile. ③

▲ This is part of a village in Côte d'Ivoire, West Africa. The round houses are made from baked mud and dried reeds. ④

▼ The Dinka people from Sudan are among the tallest peoples in the world. They spend nearly all their lives tending their herds of cattle. ⑤

◄ Dotted about the Sahara Desert are places where water gushes and palm trees grow. These are called oases. Very often towns are built at these oases, like this one in Egypt. The tall tower is a minaret. From here, a man calls people to come to the mosque for prayer. ⑥

MEDITERRANEAN SEA

GHAZI
ALEXANDRIA
CAIRO
SUEZ
Nile
EGYPT
⑥
L. Nasser
③
Y A
D E S E R T
C H A D
RED SEA
BUR SUDAN
KHARTOUM
Darfur
SUDAN
Blue Nile
White Nile
ASMERA
ERITREA
DJIBOUTI
DJIBOUTI
Ethiopian
ADDIS ABABA
Highlands
ETHIOPIA
⑤
CENTRAL AFRICAN REPUBLIC.
BANGUI
S O M A L I A
MOGADISHU

SOUTHERN AFRICA

THE SOUTHERN half of the African continent is very different from the northern half. There are rainforests, savanna grasslands and high mountain ranges.

Herds of animals still wander freely on the savannah. Giraffes, wildebeest, zebras, elephants and others move about the plains feeding on grass and leaves. Lions, cheetahs and hyenas prey on these grazing animals.

The Bantu people, herdsmen and farmers, travelled from western to southern Africa hundreds of years ago and made it their home. Europeans and Asians have also settled here.

▲ The giraffe is the tallest animal in the world. It feeds on the leaves in the trees of the savannah. ①

▲ A woman from Mozambique. She moistens her skin using cream made from crushed bark. ②

▼ The Zambezi river plunges 128 m at the Victoria Falls. To local people, the Falls are known as Mosi-oa-Tunya ("the smoke that thunders"). ⑦

▲ Poachers kill elephants and rhinos for their tusks and horns. ⑥

Scale

0   400 km

COMOROS

KENYA
L. Turkana
NAIROBI ★
MOMBASA ●
Kilimanjaro
Zanzibar
DAR ES SALAAM ●
DODOMA ★
①
UGANDA
KAMPALA ★
L. Victoria
TANZANIA
L. Nyasa
L. Albert
RWANDA
BURUNDI
BUKAVU ●
BUJUMBURA ★
L. Tanganyika
MALAWI
KISANGANI ●
Lualaba
CONGO
KANANGA ●
KATANGA
LUBUMBASHI ●
MBANDAKA ●
Congo
Ubangi
KINSHASA ★
Cuango
ANGOLA
CONGO-BRAZZAVILLE
Congo
GABON
BRAZZAVILLE ★
CABINDA (Angola)
LUANDA ★
BENGUELA ●
Bie

LIBREVILLE ★

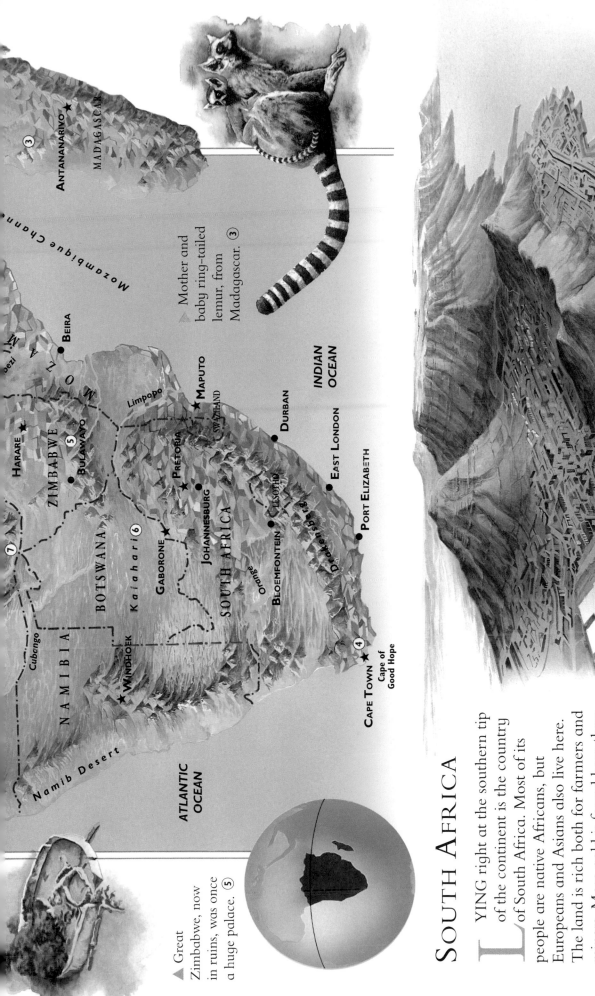

▲ Rising behind Cape Town is the flat-topped Table Mountain. ④

▲ Mother and baby ring-tailed lemur, from Madagascar. ③

ANTANANARIVO ★
MADAGASCAR ③

Mozambique Channel

INDIAN OCEAN

BEIRA ●

MAPUTO ★
SWAZILAND
Limpopo
DURBAN ●
EAST LONDON ●
PORT ELIZABETH ●

HARARE ★
ZIMBABWE ⑤
BULAWAYO ●
PRETORIA ★
JOHANNESBURG ★
LESOTHO
BLOEMFONTEIN ●
Drakensberg
Orange
SOUTH AFRICA

⑦
BOTSWANA
Kalahari ⑥
GABORONE ★

NAMIBIA
WINDHOEK ★
Cubango

Namib Desert

ATLANTIC OCEAN

CAPE TOWN ★ ④
Cape of Good Hope

▲ Great Zimbabwe, now in ruins, was once a huge palace. ⑤

SOUTH AFRICA

LYING right at the southern tip of the continent is the country of South Africa. Most of its people are native Africans, but Europeans and Asians also live here. The land is rich both for farmers and miners. More gold is found here than in any other country in the world. Near the Cape of Good Hope, the point where Atlantic and Indian Oceans meet, fruit and vines are grown. For most of the year, the weather is warm and sunny.

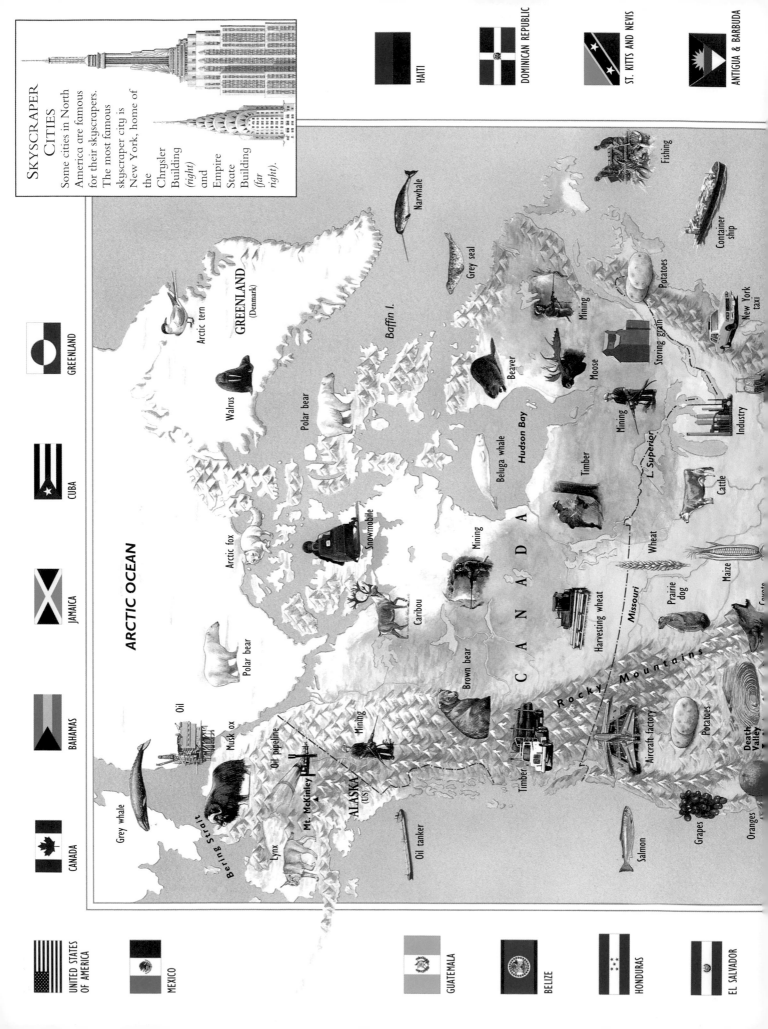

HAITI

DOMINICAN REPUBLIC

ST. KITTS AND NEVIS

ANTIGUA & BARBUDA

GREENLAND

CUBA

JAMAICA

BAHAMAS

CANADA

UNITED STATES OF AMERICA

MEXICO

GUATEMALA

BELIZE

HONDURAS

EL SALVADOR

ARCTIC OCEAN

Arctic tern

GREENLAND
(Denmark)

Narwhale

Grey seal

Fishing

Container ship

Walrus

Polar bear

Baffin I.

Mining

Potatoes

New York taxi

Storing grain

Moose

Beaver

Mining

Industry

Beluga whale

Hudson Bay

Timber

L. Superior

Cattle

Arctic fox

Mining

C A N A D A

Wheat

Maize

Snowmobile

Caribou

Harvesting wheat

Missouri

Prairie dog

Oil

Musk ox

Oil pipeline

Brown bear

Rocky Mountains

Mt. McKinley ▲

Mining

Timber

Aircraft factory

Potatoes

Death Valley

Grey whale

Bering Strait

Lynx

ALASKA
(US)

Oil tanker

Salmon

Grapes

Oranges

Polar bear

North America

NORTH AMERICA stretches from the icy Arctic islands of Greenland and northern Canada to the hot, steamy rainforests of the Caribbean coast.

Human beings first arrived in North America from Asia at least 14,000 years ago. It was the time of Ice Ages when ice sheets covered large parts of the world. The Bering Strait, which separates North America from Asia, was then dry land. The first Americans spread out across the continent and lived by hunting the animals they found there.

The first Europeans to set eyes on North America were Norsemen. About 1,000 years ago, they explored the coasts of Baffin Island and Labrador, and settled in Newfoundland. After Christopher Columbus' voyage of discovery in 1492, Spanish, English and French explorers began to travel inland.

PACIFIC OCEAN

ATLANTIC OCEAN

GULF OF MEXICO

CARIBBEAN SEA

SOUTH AMERICA

MEXICO

CUBA

BAHAMAS

HAITI

JAMAICA

DOMINICAN REP.

PUERTO RICO (US)

TRINIDAD AND TOBAGO

BELIZE

GUATEMALA

HONDURAS

EL SALVADOR

NICARAGUA

COSTA RICA

PANAMA

Mississippi

Kangaroo rat

Brown pelicans diving

Sidewinder

Mining

Maize

Coffee

Herding cattle

Gas

Oil

Cotton

Tobacco

Alligator

Fishing

Shrimps

Space Shuttle launch

Cutting sugar cane

Mining

Cocoa

Toucan

Bananas

Panama Canal

Tourism

NICARAGUA

COSTA RICA

PANAMA

TRINIDAD & TOBAGO

GRENADA

ST. VINCENT AND THE GRENADINES

BARBADOS

ST. LUCIA

DOMINICA

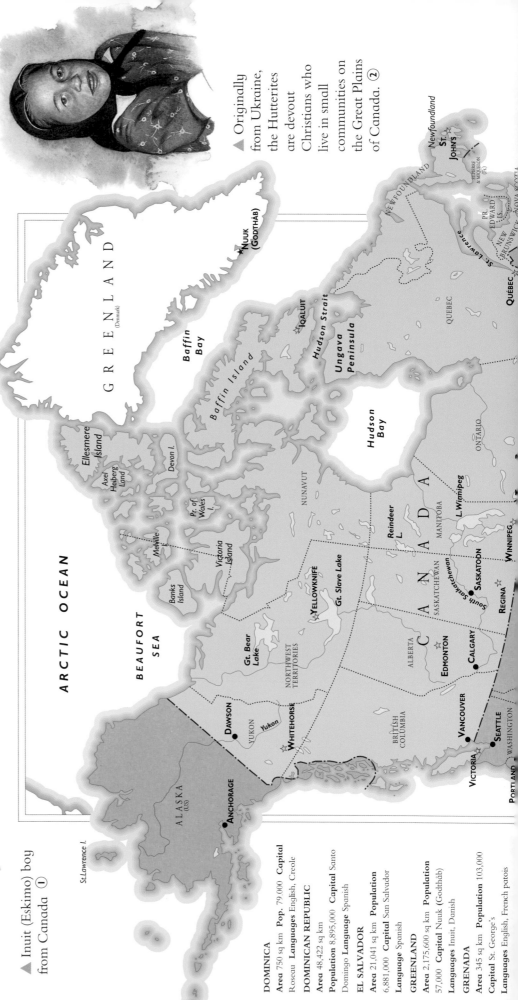

NATIONS OF NORTH AMERICA

ANGUILLA
Area 91 sq km **Population** 12,000
Capital The Valley **Language** English

ANTIGUA AND BARBUDA
Area 442 sq km **Population** 81,000
Capital St. John's **Language** English

BAHAMAS
Area 13,939 sq km **Population** 323,000
Capital Nassau **Language** English

BARBADOS
Area 430 sq km **Population** 270,000
Capital Bridgetown **Language** English

BELIZE
Area 22,965 sq km **Population** 270,000
Capital Belmopan **Languages** English, Spanish

BERMUDA
Area 53 sq km **Population** 64,000
Capital Hamilton **Language** English

BRITISH VIRGIN ISLANDS
Area 153 sq km **Population** 22,000
Capital Road Town **Language** English

CANADA
Area 9,958,319 sq km **Population** 32,268,000
Capital Ottawa **Languages** English, French

COSTA RICA
Area 50,700 sq km **Population** 4,327,000
Capital San José **Language** Spanish

CUBA
Area 110,860 sq km **Population** 11,269,000
Capital Havana **Language** Spanish

DOMINICA
Area 750 sq km **Pop.** 79,000 **Capital**
Roseau **Languages** English, Creole

DOMINICAN REPUBLIC
Area 48,422 sq km
Population 8,895,000 **Capital** Santo
Domingo **Language** Spanish

EL SALVADOR
Area 21,041 sq km **Population**
6,881,000 **Capital** San Salvador
Language Spanish

GREENLAND
Area 2,175,600 sq km **Population**
57,000 **Capital** Nuuk (Godthåb)
Languages Inuit, Danish

GRENADA
Area 345 sq km **Population** 103,000
Capital St. George's
Languages English, French patois

▲ Inuit (Eskimo) boy from Canada ①

▲ Originally from Ukraine, the Hutterites are devout Christians who live in small communities on the Great Plains of Canada. ②

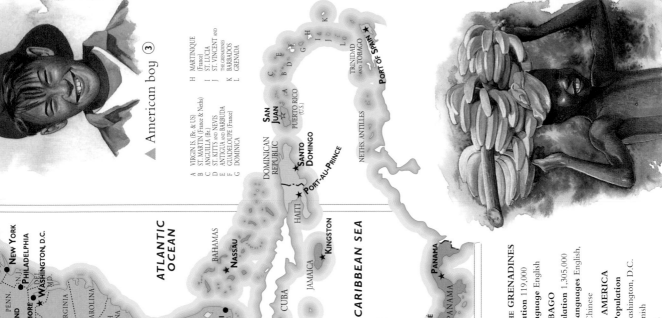

▲ American boy ③

A VIRGIN IS. (Br. & US)
B ST. MARTIN (France & Neths)
C ANGUILLA (Br.)
D ST. KITTS and NEVIS
E ANTIGUA and BARBUDA
F GUADELOUPE (France)
G DOMINICA

H MARTINIQUE (France)
I ST. LUCIA
J ST. VINCENT AND THE GRENADINES
K BARBADOS
L GRENADA

▲ Boy from Caribbean Islands ④

ATLANTIC OCEAN

CARIBBEAN SEA

PACIFIC OCEAN

Gulf of Mexico

Gulf of California

Scale

0 ——————— 800 km

★ Capital city

☆ Provincial capital

MEXICO
Area 1,972,547 sq km Population 107,029,000 Capital Mexico City
Language Spanish

MONTSERRAT
Area 102 sq km Population 5,000
Capital Plymouth Language English

NETHERLANDS ANTILLES
Area 800 sq km Population 183,000
Capital Willemstad Languages Dutch, Papiamento

NICARAGUA
Area 130,000 sq km Population 5,487,000
Capital Managua Languages Spanish, English

PANAMA
Area 75,517 sq km Population 3,232,000
Capital Panama Language Spanish

PUERTO RICO
Area 8,959 sq km Population 3,955,000
Capital San Juan Languages Spanish, English

ST. KITTS AND NEVIS
Area 262 sq km Population 43,000
Capital Basseterre Language English

ST. LUCIA
Area 616 sq km Population 161,000
Capital Castries Languages English, French patois

ST. VINCENT AND THE GRENADINES
Area 388 sq km Population 119,000
Capital Kingstown Language English

TRINIDAD AND TOBAGO
Area 5,127 sq km Population 1,305,000
Capital Port of Spain Languages English, French, Spanish, Hindi, Chinese

UNITED STATES OF AMERICA
Area 9,372,614 sq km Population 298,213,000 Capital Washington, D.C.
Languages English, Spanish

US VIRGIN ISLANDS
Area 355 sq km Population 112,000
Capital Charlotte Amalie Languages English, Spanish, Creole

▲ Guatemalan girl ⑤

▲ Hopi girl ⑥

GUADELOUPE
Area 1,779 sq km Capital Basse-Terre
448,000 Population
Languages French, Creole

GUATEMALA
Area 108,889 sq km Population 12,599,000 Capital Guatemala
Language Spanish

HAITI
Area 27,750 sq km Population 8,528,000 Capital Port-au-Prince
Languages French, Creole

HONDURAS
Area 112,088 sq km Population 7,205,000 Capital Tegucigalpa
Language Spanish

JAMAICA
Area 10,991 sq km Pop. 2,651,000
Capital Kingston Language English

MARTINIQUE
Area 1,102 sq km Population 359,000 Capital Fort-de-France
Languages French, Creole

62

CANADA

CANADA is the second largest country in the world after Russia. It is a land of high mountains in the west, forests and lakes in the centre and frozen, treeless wastes in the Arctic north. Canada's cities and farmland are situated in the south, close to the border with the United States of America.

▲ This is the face of a bear. You can see its wild eyes, fearsome teeth and flared nostrils! It was carved on a totem pole by Native Americans from British Columbia. Each pole has several carvings, one on top of the other. ⑥

◀ The wheat fields of Alberta and Saskatchewan are known as the "prairies". The harvested grain is stored in elevators like these. ①

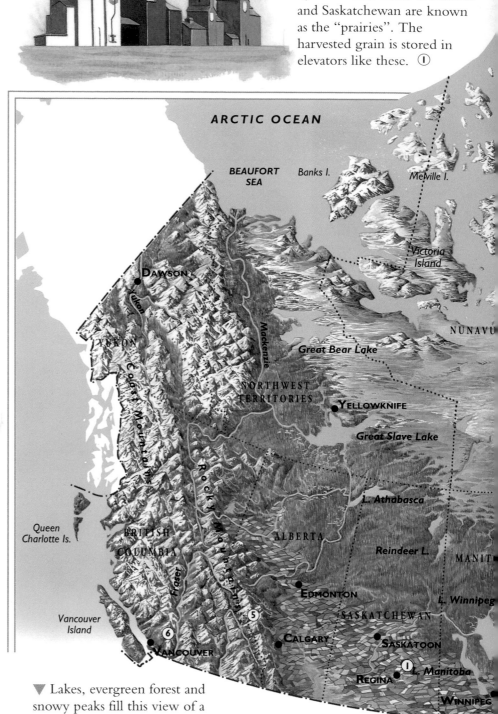

ARCTIC OCEAN

BEAUFORT SEA
Banks I.
Melville I.
Victoria Island
NUNAVU
DAWSON
Yukon
YUKON
Coast Mountains
Mackenzie
Great Bear Lake
NORTHWEST TERRITORIES
YELLOWKNIFE
Great Slave Lake
L. Athabasca
Rocky Mountains
ALBERTA
Reindeer L.
MANIT
Queen Charlotte Is.
BRITISH COLUMBIA
Fraser
EDMONTON
L. Winnipeg
Vancouver Island
⑤
⑥
CALGARY
SASKATCHEWAN
SASKATOON
VANCOUVER
① L. Manitoba
REGINA
L. Manitoba
WINNIPEG

▼ Lakes, evergreen forest and snowy peaks fill this view of a valley in the Rocky Mountains. ⑤

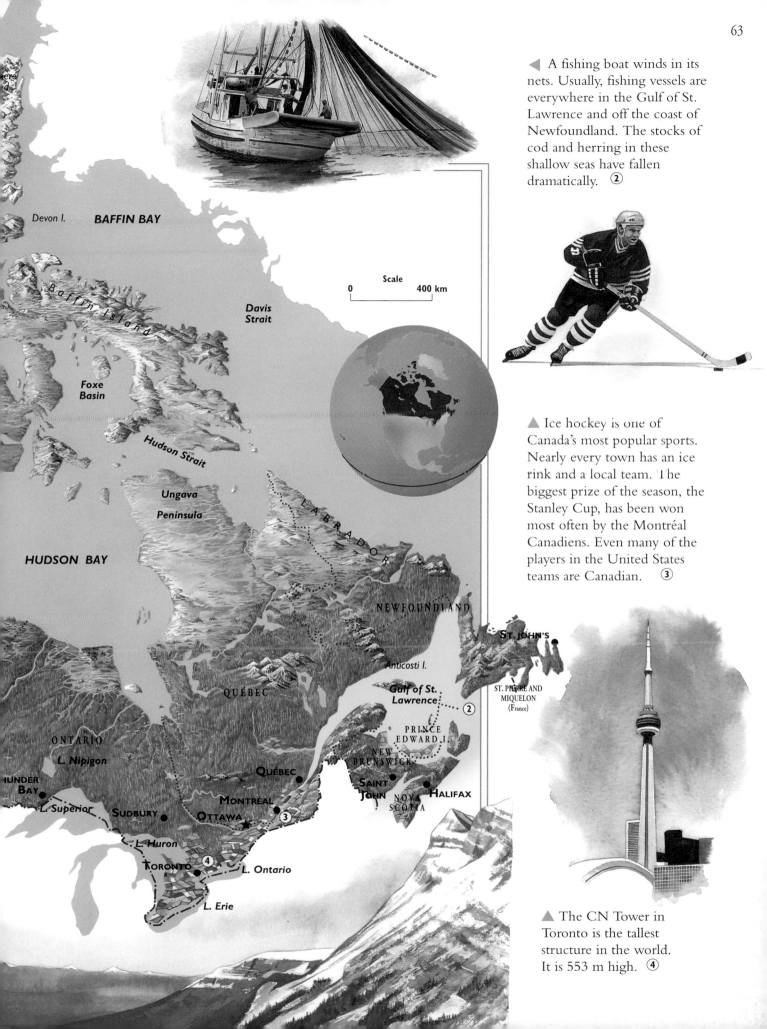

◀ A fishing boat winds in its nets. Usually, fishing vessels are everywhere in the Gulf of St. Lawrence and off the coast of Newfoundland. The stocks of cod and herring in these shallow seas have fallen dramatically. ②

▲ Ice hockey is one of Canada's most popular sports. Nearly every town has an ice rink and a local team. The biggest prize of the season, the Stanley Cup, has been won most often by the Montréal Canadiens. Even many of the players in the United States teams are Canadian. ③

▲ The CN Tower in Toronto is the tallest structure in the world. It is 553 m high. ④

Scale
0   400 km

Devon I.   **BAFFIN BAY**

Baffin Island

Davis Strait

Foxe Basin

Hudson Strait

Ungava Peninsula

LABRADOR

HUDSON BAY

NEWFOUNDLAND

ST. JOHN'S

Anticosti I.

QUÉBEC

Gulf of St. Lawrence ②

ST. PIERRE AND MIQUELON (France)

PRINCE EDWARD I.

NEW BRUNSWICK

ONTARIO

L. Nipigon

THUNDER BAY

L. Superior

SUDBURY

QUÉBEC

MONTRÉAL

OTTAWA ③

SAINT JOHN

NOVA SCOTIA

HALIFAX

TORONTO ④

L. Huron

L. Ontario

L. Erie

UNITED STATES

THE United States of America consists of 50 states, including Hawaii and Alaska.

East of the Rocky Mountains, vast farmlands stretch away as far as the eye can see. Sprawling cities cluster together in the northeastern states. West of the Rockies, much of the land inland from the Pacific coast is desert.

▲ The trunk of this giant sequoia tree in California is so thick cars can drive through it! One tree of this kind, known as "General Sherman," is the most massive living thing in the world. ⑥

VT.	VERMONT
N.H.	NEW HAMPSHIRE
MASS.	MASSACHUSETTS
CONN.	CONNECTICUT
R.I.	RHODE ISLAND
N.J.	NEW JERSEY
MD.	MARYLAND
DEL.	DELAWARE

Scale
0   400 km

▼ Much of the southwestern USA is desert. Some spectacular landscapes, like Monument Valley in Arizona, are found here. ⑤

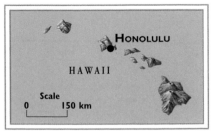

HAWAII

HONOLULU

Scale
0   150 km

◀ The Golden Gate Bridge crosses the entrance to San Francisco Bay. ①

◀ The Gateway Arch, in St. Louis, Missouri, is the tallest monument in the world. It was built to mark the city's historic role as "gateway to the West". Wagon trains once set out from here on their way to California. The Arch is hollow. Inside, lifts go up to a viewing platform at the top. ②

▲ The United States Capitol in Washington, D.C., is one of the most famous landmarks in the world. Congress is the US parliament. It consists of the House of Representatives and the Senate, both of which meet inside this building. ③

▲ This is a club in New Orleans, Louisiana, where jazz musicians are performing. New Orleans is the home of jazz, a style of music invented by black musicians in the early years of the 20th century. ④

STATES OF THE USA

ALABAMA
Area 135,775 sq km **Population** 4,558,000
Capital Montgomery **Largest city** Birmingham

ALASKA
Area 1,700,139 sq km **Population** 664,000
Capital Juneau **Largest city** Anchorage

ARIZONA
Area 295,267 sq km **Population** 5,939,000
Capital and largest city Phoenix

ARKANSAS
Area 137,742 sq km **Population** 2,779,000
Capital and largest city Little Rock

CALIFORNIA
Area 424,002 sq km **Population** 36,132,000
Capital Sacramento **Largest city** Los Angeles

COLORADO
Area 269,620 sq km **Population** 4,665,000
Capital and largest city Denver

CONNECTICUT
Area 14,358 sq km **Population** 3,510,000
Capital Hartford **Largest city** Bridgeport

KANSAS
Area 213,110 sq km **Population** 2,745,000
Capital Topeka **Largest city** Wichita

KENTUCKY
Area 104,665 sq km **Population** 4,173,000
Capital Frankfort **Largest city** Louisville

MAINE
Area 91,653 sq km **Population** 1,322,000
Capital Augusta **Largest city** Portland

MARYLAND
Area 32,135 sq km **Population** 5,600,000
Capital Annapolis **Largest city** Baltimore

▶ Hoover Dam ①

▲ Bucking bronco at a rodeo ⑥

DELAWARE
Area 6,447 sq km **Population** 844,000
Capital Dover **Largest city** Wilmington

FLORIDA
Area 170,313 sq km **Population** 17,790,000
Capital Tallahassee **Largest city** Jacksonville

GEORGIA
Area 153,953 sq km **Population** 9,073,000
Capital and largest city Atlanta

HAWAII
Area 28,313 sq km **Population** 1,275,000
Capital and largest city Honolulu

IDAHO
Area 216,456 sq km **Population** 1,429,000
Capital and largest city Boise

ILLINOIS
Area 150,007 sq km **Population** 12,763,000
Capital Springfield **Largest city** Chicago

INDIANA
Area 94,328 sq km **Population** 6,272,000
Capital and largest city Indianapolis

IOWA
Area 145,754 sq km **Population** 2,966,000
Capital and largest city Des Moines

LOUISIANA
Area 134,275 sq km **Population** 4,524,000 **Capital** Baton Rouge **Largest city** New Orleans

MASSACHUSETTS
Area 27,337 sq km **Population** 6,399,000 **Capital and largest city** Boston

PACIFIC OCEAN

ARCTIC OCEAN

BARROW

St. Lawrence I.

Yukon

ALASKA

ANCHORAGE

Kodiak I.

JUNEAU

Aleutian Islands

Scale

0   400 km

Scale

0   400 km

MICHIGAN
Area 250,738 sq km Population 10,121,000
Capital Lansing Largest city Detroit

MINNESOTA
Area 225,182 sq km Population 5,133,000
Capital St. Paul Largest city Minneapolis

MISSISSIPPI
Area 125,443 sq km Population 2,921,000
Capital and largest city Jackson

NEW HAMPSHIRE
Area 24,219 sq km Population 1,310,000
Capital Concord Largest city Manchester

NEW JERSEY
Area 22,590 sq km Population 8,718,000
Capital Trenton Largest city Newark

NEW MEXICO
Area 314,939 sq km Population 1,928,000
Capital Santa Fe Largest city Albuquerque

NEW YORK
Area 141,089 sq km Population 19,254,000
Capital Albany Largest city New York

NORTH CAROLINA
Area 139,397 sq km Population 8,683,000
Capital Raleigh Largest city Charlotte

NORTH DAKOTA
Area 183,123 sq km Population 637,000
Capital Bismarck Largest city Fargo

OHIO
Area 116,103 sq km Population 11,464,000
Capital and largest city Columbus

OKLAHOMA
Area 181,049 sq km Population 3,548,000
Capital and largest city Oklahoma City

OREGON
Area 254,819 sq km Population 3,641,000
Capital Salem Largest city Portland

PENNSYLVANIA
Area 119,291 sq km Population 12,430,000
Capital Harrisburg Largest city Philadelphia

RHODE ISLAND
Area 4,002 sq km Population 1,076,000
Capital and largest city Providence

SOUTH CAROLINA
Area 82,898 sq km Population 4,255,000
Capital and largest city Columbia

SOUTH DAKOTA
Area 199,745 sq km Population 756,000
Capital Pierre Largest city Sioux Falls

TENNESSEE
Area 109,158 sq km Population 5,963,000
Capital Nashville Largest city Memphis

TEXAS
Area 695,676 sq km Population 22,860,000
Capital Austin Largest city Houston

UTAH
Area 219,902 sq km Population 2,470,000
Capital and largest city Salt Lake City

▲ The Fall in New England ②

▲ Whale-watching ③

VERMONT
Area 24,903 sq km Population 623,000
Capital Montpelier Largest city Burlington

VIRGINIA
Area 110,771 sq km Population 7,567,000
Capital Richmond Largest city Virginia Beach

WASHINGTON
Area 184,674 sq km Population 6,288,000
Capital Olympia Largest city Seattle

WEST VIRGINIA
Area 62,759 sq km Population 1,817,000
Capital and largest city Charleston

WISCONSIN
Area 169,653 sq km Population 5,536,000
Capital Madison Largest city Milwaukee

WYOMING
Area 253,349 sq km Population 509,000
Capital and largest city Cheyenne

VT.   VERMONT
N.H. NEW HAMPSHIRE
CONN. CONNECTICUT
R.I. RHODE ISLAND
N.J. NEW JERSEY
DEL. DELAWARE
MD.   MARYLAND

★ Capital city
☆ State capital

Scale
0   150 km

ATLANTIC OCEAN

Gulf of Mexico

MISSOURI
Area 180,546 sq km Pop. 5,800,000 Capital Jefferson City Largest city Kansas City

MONTANA
Area 380,850 sq km Population 936,000
Capital Helena Largest city Billings

NEBRASKA
Area 200,358 sq km Population 1,759,000
Capital Lincoln Largest city Omaha

NEVADA
Area 286,368 sq km Population 2,415,000
Capital Carson City Largest city Las Vegas

◄ Cliff Palace ⑤

► The Statue of Liberty ④

MEXICO
AND CENTRAL AMERICA

IN northern Mexico, mountain chains run down both coastlines. The high, flat land between them is dry and dusty, dotted with low bushes called scrub. Farther south, in Central America, the land narrows and the climate becomes more tropical.

◀ A colourful tree frog from Central America. ①

▲ This is a volcano in Costa Rica. Smoke drifts gently from the crater at its summit. Sometimes, often without warning, a volcano will erupt. In a huge explosion, great clouds of dust and ash fill the sky. Lava, rock that is so hot it flows like a liquid, cascades down the mountainside. There are many volcanoes in Mexico and Central America. ⑥

MEXICALI

CIUDAD JUÁREZ

Rio Grande

Baja California

CULIACÁN

MONTERREY

M E X I C O

GULF OF MEXICO

GUADALAJARA

MEXICO CITY ★

VERACRUZ

Yucatán Peninsula

ME
⑤

VILLAHERMOSA

BELMOPAN

GUATEMALA
GUATEMALA ★

SAN SALVADOR ★
EL SALVADOR

Scale

0   600 km

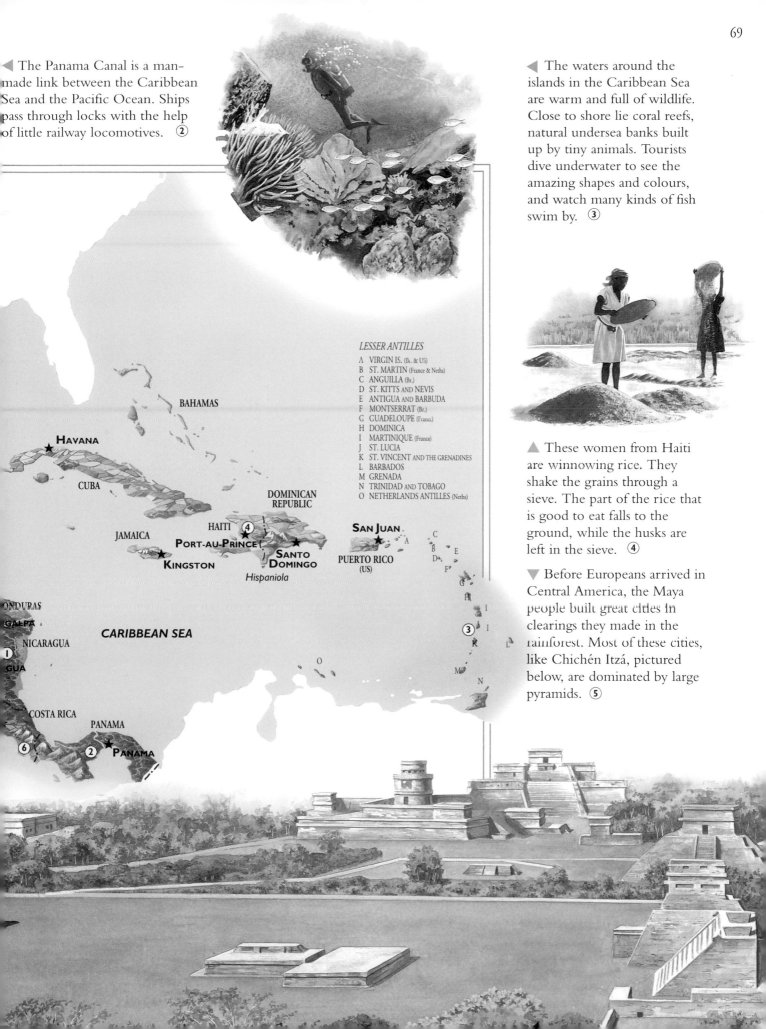

◀ The Panama Canal is a man-made link between the Caribbean Sea and the Pacific Ocean. Ships pass through locks with the help of little railway locomotives. ②

◀ The waters around the islands in the Caribbean Sea are warm and full of wildlife. Close to shore lie coral reefs, natural undersea banks built up by tiny animals. Tourists dive underwater to see the amazing shapes and colours, and watch many kinds of fish swim by. ③

▲ These women from Haiti are winnowing rice. They shake the grains through a sieve. The part of the rice that is good to eat falls to the ground, while the husks are left in the sieve. ④

▼ Before Europeans arrived in Central America, the Maya people built great cities in clearings they made in the rainforest. Most of these cities, like Chichén Itzá, pictured below, are dominated by large pyramids. ⑤

BAHAMAS

LESSER ANTILLES
A VIRGIN IS. (Br. & US)
B ST. MARTIN (France & Neths)
C ANGUILLA (Br.)
D ST. KITTS AND NEVIS
E ANTIGUA AND BARBUDA
F MONTSERRAT (Br.)
G GUADELOUPE (France)
H DOMINICA
I MARTINIQUE (France)
J ST. LUCIA
K ST. VINCENT AND THE GRENADINES
L BARBADOS
M GRENADA
N TRINIDAD AND TOBAGO
O NETHERLANDS ANTILLES (Neths)

HAVANA
CUBA
JAMAICA
Kingston
Port-au-Prince
HAITI
DOMINICAN REPUBLIC
SANTO DOMINGO
Hispaniola
SAN JUAN
PUERTO RICO (US)
ONDURAS
GALPA
NICARAGUA
CARIBBEAN SEA
COSTA RICA
PANAMA
PANAMA

BRAZIL

 ECUADOR

 PERU

 BOLIVIA

 PARAGUAY

 URUGUAY

 ARGENTINA

 CHILE

 FRENCH GUIANA

 SURINAME

GUYANA

VENEZUELA

COLOMBIA

SOUTH AMERICA

SOUTH AMERICA reaches from the tropical coast of the Caribbean to the icy seas of the Southern Ocean. It is joined to North America by a thin neck of land, known as the Isthmus of Panama.

Most of South America's population lives in the east of the continent. Apart from the Guianas and Brazil (where Portuguese is spoken) Spanish is the main language. Much of South America was once under Spanish rule. The people themselves are descended from the native Indians, Spanish and Portuguese settlers, later immigrants from other parts of Europe, and Africans.

FACTS ABOUT SOUTH AMERICA

Area 17,663,000 sq km
Population 375,185,000
Highest point Aconcagua (Argentina) 6,960 m
Lowest point Salinas Chicas (Argentina) 42 m below sea level
Longest river Amazon 6,451 km
Largest lake Titicaca (Peru and Bolivia) 8,340 sq km
Largest country Brazil 8,511,996 sq km
Largest population Brazil 186,405,000
Largest city São Paulo (Brazil) 18,300,000 people

ATLANTIC OCEAN

Equator

Oil

Cattle

VENEZUELA

Mining

FRENCH GUIANA

SURINAME

GUYANA

Giant anteater

COLOMBIA

Coffee

Sloth

ECUADOR

Cocoa

Mining

Fishing

Potatoes

PERU

Jaguar

BOLIVIA

Hummingbird

Amazon

Spider monkey

Anaconda

Capybara

Piranha

BRAZIL

Mining

Vampire bat

Armadillo

Sugar cane

Bananas

Cocoa

Manatee

 ▲ Amazon Indian girl

 ▲ Indian girl from the Andes, Bolivia ③

NATIONS OF SOUTH AMERICA

ARGENTINA
Area 2,766,889 sq km **Population** 38,747,000
Capital Buenos Aires **Language** Spanish

BOLIVIA
Area 1,098,581 sq km **Population** 9,182,000
Capitals La Paz, Sucre **Languages** Spanish,
Quechua, Aymara

BRAZIL
Area 8,511,996 sq km **Population**
186,405,000 **Capital** Brasilia **Language**
Portuguese

CHILE
Area 756,626 sq km **Population** 16,295,000
Capital Santiago **Language** Spanish

COLOMBIA
Area 1,141,748 sq km **Population** 45,600,000
Capital Bogotá **Language** Spanish

ECUADOR
Area 272,045 sq km **Population** 13,228,000
Capital Quito **Languages** Spanish, Quechua

FALKLAND ISLANDS
Area 12,173 sq km **Population** 3,000
Capital Stanley **Language** English

FRENCH GUIANA
Area 91,000 sq km **Pop.** 187,000
Capital Cayenne **Languages** French, Creole

GUYANA
Area 214,969 sq km **Population** 751,000
Capital Georgetown **Languages** English,
Hindi, Urdu

PARAGUAY
Area 406,752 sq km **Population** 5,158,000
Capital Asunción **Languages** Spanish, Guaraní

PERU
Area 1,285,216 sq km **Population** 27,965,000
Capital Lima **Languages** Spanish, Quechua,
Aymara

SURINAME
Area 163,265 sq km **Pop.** 449,000 **Capital**
Paramaribo **Languages** Dutch, Hindi, Javanese

URUGUAY
Area 176,215 sq km **Population** 3,463,000
Capital Montevideo **Language** Spanish

VENEZUELA
Area 912,050 sq km **Population** 26,749,300
Capital Caracas **Language** Spanish

▲ Chilean boy ②

RAINFOREST

The Amazon rainforest is the largest in the world. Many trees are being felled to make way for farms, roads and quarries. The survival of the forest wildlife and peoples is threatened. Some scientists think the world's climate may be affected by this as well.

Scale 1000 km

★ Capital city

0

FALKLAND IS. (Br.)

Industry

Hydro-electric dam

Soya beans

Herding cattle

Cattle

URUGUAY

PARAGUAY

Puma

Herding llama

Maize

ARGENTINA

Rhea

Salinas Chicas

Sheep

Condor

Aconcagua

Andes

Grapes

Mining

CHILE

harvester

FALKLAND IS. (Br.)

BRAZIL

Tocantins

Paraná

Madeira

Amazon

PERU

Cuzco

Arequipa

Antofagasta

La Paz

BOLIVIA

Sucre

Asunción

PARAGUAY

Córdoba

Rosario

Santiago

Valparaíso

Concepción

ARGENTINA

Bahía Blanca

Buenos Aires

Montevideo

URUGUAY

Equator

Orinoco

VENEZUELA

Caracas

Maracaibo

Medellín

Bogotá

Cali

COLOMBIA

Quito

ECUADOR

Guayaquil

Iquitos

Trujillo

Lima

Manaus

Belém

Fortaleza

Recife

Salvador

Belo Horizonte

Brasília

Rio de Janeiro

São Paulo

Porto Alegre

Georgetown

Paramaribo

Cayenne

FRENCH GUIANA

GUYANA

SURINAME

E

BRAZIL AND ITS NEIGHBOURS

LYING across the centre of this map is a huge river basin. It looks as if an enormous green blanket has been laid across it. This is the Amazon Rainforest. Hundreds of different kinds of birds and animals live here.

Around the rim of the basin are highlands. (Turn to pages 74–75 to see a map of the Andes, the mountains which form the western edge.) Many great rivers start out as tiny streams in these highlands. They all snake through the forest to meet the mighty Amazon. This vast river carries a fifth of all the world's fresh water into the Atlantic Ocean.

Few people inhabit the Amazon region. Most Brazilians live in the crowded cities of the southeast.

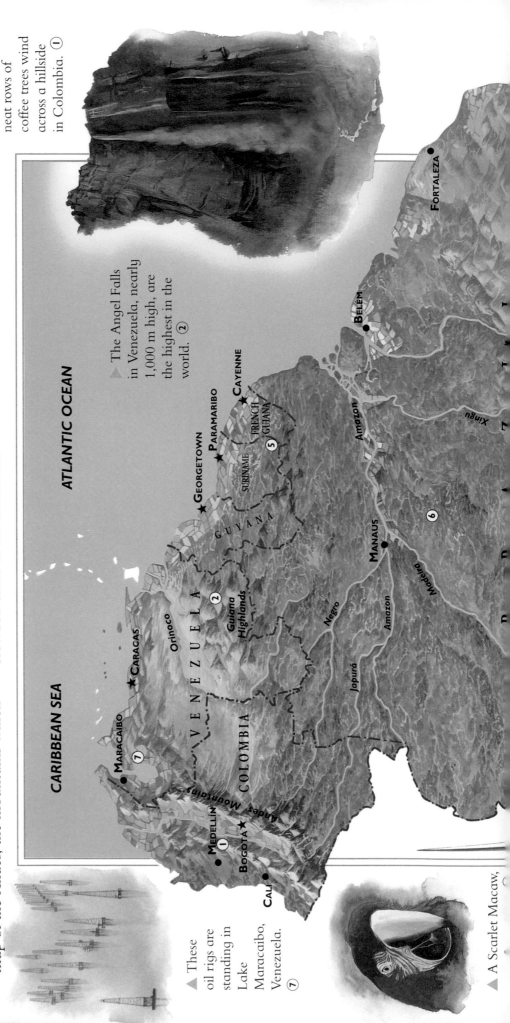

▲ Hundreds of neat rows of coffee trees wind across a hillside in Colombia. ①

▲ The Angel Falls in Venezuela, nearly 1,000 m high, are the highest in the world. ②

CARIBBEAN SEA

ATLANTIC OCEAN

FORTALEZA

BELÉM

Xingu

Amazon

CAYENNE

PARAMARIBO

FRENCH GUIANA

SURINAME ⑤

GEORGETOWN

GUYANA

MANAUS

Madeira

Amazon

⑥

Guiana Highlands ②

Negro

Japurá

Amazon

CARACAS

Orinoco

VENEZUELA

MARACAIBO ⑦

COLOMBIA

Andes Mountains

MEDELLÍN ①

BOGOTÁ

CALI

▲ These oil rigs are standing in Lake Maracaibo, Venezuela. ⑦

▲ A Scarlet Macaw,

▲ A dancer at a Rio de Janeiro carnival. ③

Scale

0   400 km

▼ In January 1503 a Portuguese explorer called Gonçalo Coelho sailed his ship into a Brazilian bay. He mistakenly thought he had found the mouth of a great river, so he called it the January River—or, in his own language, Rio de Janeiro.

A great city has since grown up around the shores of that beautiful bay. The Sugar Loaf mountain, shaped like a rounded cone, overlooks its harbour. Rich people live in luxury apartments with wonderful views. Poor people live in shabby slums on the edge of the city. Their shantytowns are known as the *favelas*. ④

▲ The Amazon Rainforest is home to many native peoples. But more and more of them are leaving to live and work in the towns. Their old ways of life may soon be lost forever. ⑤

SALVADOR

BELO HORIZONTE

São Fran

BRASÍLIA ★

CAMPINAS

③ ④ RIO DE JANEIRO

SÃO PAULO

Paraná

CURITIBA

PORTO ALEGRE

74

THE ANDES

THE ANDES mountains run from top to bottom of this map. In Ecuador, Peru and parts of Bolivia, tropical rainforests cling to their eastern slopes. Over on the western side, where the mountains rise behind the Pacific coast, there are not even any trees—just desert. Some parts have not felt rain for more than 400 years!

Until the Spanish conquerors first arrived in Peru 1524, the mighty Inca emperor reigned supreme over this land. Today, the Indians still speak Quechua, the language of the Incas. Some Indians still farm the steep hillsides of the Andes and graze their llamas and alpacas on the high plains.

▲ The Spanish invaders never found Machu Picchu. This Inca city was built high in the mountains. It was "lost" to the rest of the world until 1911. ②

(above, left) For hundreds of years, people have crossed the deep gorges in the Andes by rope bridges. ①

▲ The Galápagos Islands are famous for their wildlife, like this giant tortoise. ⑦

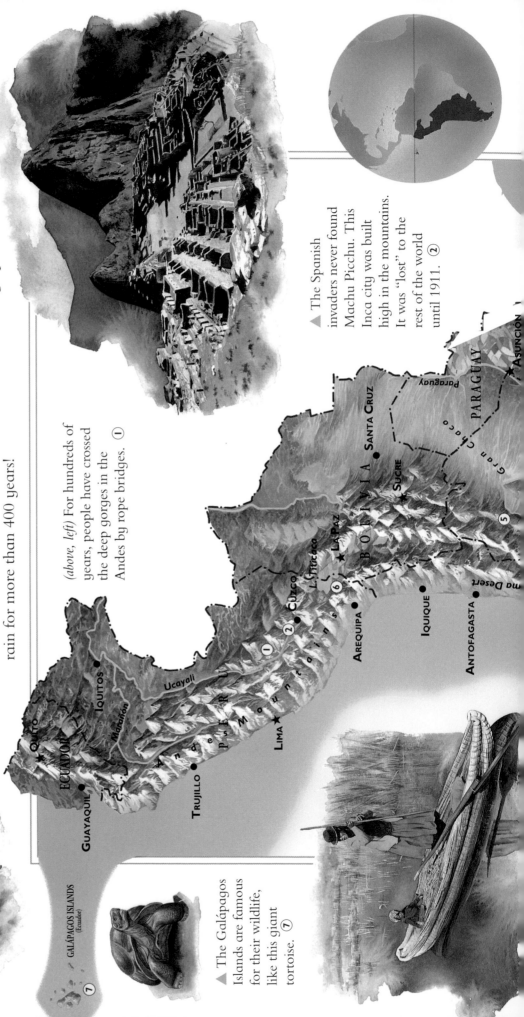

GALÁPAGOS ISLANDS
(Ecuador) ⑦

ECUADOR
QUITO ★
GUAYAQUIL ●
IQUITOS ●
Marañón
Ucayali

P E R U
Andes Mountains
TRUJILLO ●
LIMA ★
CUZCO ● ②
①
L. Titicaca
⑥
LA PAZ ★
AREQUIPA ●
IQUIQUE ●
ANTOFAGASTA ●
__ma Desert

B O L I V I A
SUCRE ★
SANTA CRUZ ●
⑤
Gran Chaco
PARAGUAY
Paraguay
ASUNCIÓN ★

▶ Few gauchos herd cattle on the Argentinian pampas on horseback nowadays. ③

ATLANTIC OCEAN

▶ Guanacos live in the remote mountains of southern Chile. ④

URUGUAY
SANTA FE
MONTEVIDEO ★
CORDOBA
ROSARIO
Río de la Plata
BUENOS AIRES ★
③
Aconcagua
MENDOZA
MAR DEL PLATA
ARGENTINA
SANTIAGO ★
BAHÍA BLANCA
P a m p a s
VALPARAÍSO
C H I L E
Andes Mountains
COMODORO RIVADAVIA
CONCEPCIÓN
P A T A G O N I A
④
FALKLAND ISLANDS (Br.)
Magellan's Strait
Tierra del Fuego
Cape Horn

PACIFIC OCEAN

Scale
0 — 400 km

woman steers a reed boat across Lake Titicaca, the highest lake in the world. ⑥

▲ The "Train of the Clouds" crosses a high viaduct in the Andes. ⑤

CHILE AND ARGENTINA

A BORDER threads its way from peak to peak in the southern Andes. To the west lies Chile, a long, thin country, 25 times longer than it is wide. To the east lies Argentina, its fertile, grassy plains turning into the dry and dusty Patagonian desert in the south. The island of Tierra del Fuego (the "land of fire," named after the Indian camp fires sighted by the Portuguese explorer Magellan) lies at South America's southern tip.

THE POLES

BOTH the North Pole in the Arctic and the South Pole in the Antarctic are bitterly cold places, covered with ice and snow all year round. The Arctic is quite different from the Antarctic in one important way. It is not land at all, but an ocean covered by a vast, frozen cap of thick ice. Antarctica is a continent, like Asia or Africa. Beneath the ice, more than 3,500 metres deep in places, there is land.

▲ Ships sail through Arctic waters every day. Icebreakers carve a passage for them through the rafts of floating ice, called pack ice. ⑦

▼ Emperor penguins gather together on an Antarctic shore. Floating out to sea is an iceberg, a block of ice that has broken away from the ice shelf. ⑥

◀ This is a walrus, an Arctic seal with tusks. When out of the water, walruses huddle together in their hundreds. ①

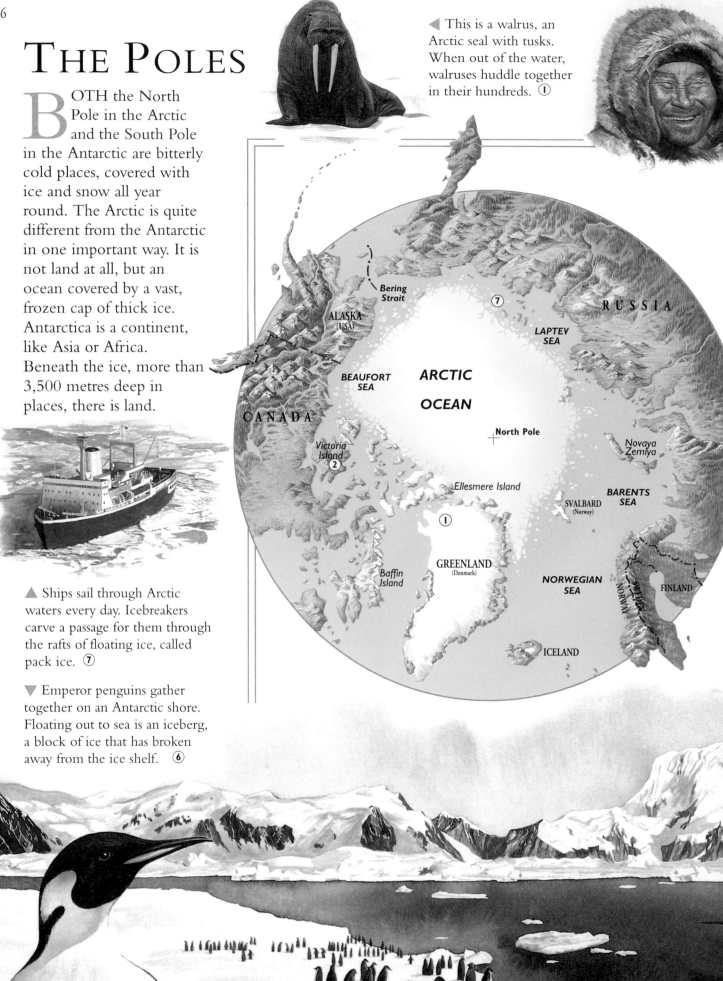

ALASKA (USA)
Bering Strait
BEAUFORT SEA
CANADA
Victoria Island ②
ARCTIC OCEAN
North Pole
Ellesmere Island
①
Baffin Island
GREENLAND (Denmark)
⑦
RUSSIA
LAPTEV SEA
Novaya Zemlya
SVALBARD (Norway)
BARENTS SEA
NORWEGIAN SEA
NORWAY
SWEDEN
FINLAND
ICELAND

◀ The Inuit, from Greenland and northern Canada, are one of many Arctic peoples who inhabit the shores of the Arctic Ocean. Some still live by hunting walruses, seals and whales. ②

◀ The Poles were first reached by people less than 100 years ago. An American, Robert Peary, was first to the North Pole in 1909. Norwegian explorer Roald Amundsen beat a British expedition led by Robert F. Scott to the South Pole in 1911. This picture shows a modern polar explorer. His team of husky dogs pulls his sled laden with provisions. ③

▲ The humpback whale can flip right out of the water, a leap known as "breaching". The humpback is famous for its underwater singing. ④

▲ At the South Pole today there is a research station. Scientists live and work here all year round. ⑤

WEDDELL SEA

Antarctic Peninsula

QUEEN MAUD LAND

④

⑥

BELLINGSHAUSEN SEA

ANTARCTICA

③

South Pole
⑤

BYRD LAND

Ross Ice Shelf

WILKES LAND

ROSS SEA

Scale
0   500 km

SOUTHERN OCEAN

PICTURE INDEX

MAP INDEX